AN ESTANCIA IN PATAGONIA
NORA MACKINNON

AN ESTANCIA IN PATAGONIA
NORA MACKINNON

 L.O.L.A. Literature of Latin America

Copyright © 2003 by L.O.L.A. (Literature of
Latin America). Todos los derechos reservados

http://www.lola-online.com

Librería: Viamonte 976 - 2º piso Dto. D.
C1053ABT Buenos Aires,
República Argentina
Tel.: 4322-3920 / 4322-4577
Fax: (+54 11) 4372-2787

Editorial responsable: Colin Sharp
Rodríguez Peña 115
C1020ADC Buenos Aires,
República Argentina.
Tel.: (+54 11) 4372-0518
Fax: (+54 11) 4372-2787
E-mail: csharp@ba.net

I.S.B.N. 950-9725-55-2

Impreso en: Los Talleres Gráficos LUX S.A.
H. Yrigoyen 2463 - S3000BLE Santa Fe.

Buenos Aires, Argentina, Noviembre de 2003

Cita bibliográfica:
Nora Mackinnon (2003)
An Estancia In Patagonia.
L.O.L.A., Buenos Aires, Argentina, 186 págs.

Acknowledgements

I would like to thank Andrew Graham-Yooll, Senior Editor of the Buenos Aires Herald, for his advice and encouragement; Anthony Traill for the time he spent and the trouble he took in the early stages of finding a publisher; Lidia Ceriana for helping me with the glossary and Renee Benitz for putting the book on a disc.

I would also like to thank Mr and Mrs Vernon Gallup, Rhianon Gough, the Australian Mackinnons, Jane and Michael Beale and my family for their help and affection.

Contents

CHIRU

BUENOS AIRES

NEUQUEN

BAHIA BLANCA

SAN JOSE

AGUADA GUZMAN

ALICURA

OSORNO

PASO FLORES

PILCANIYEU

PATAGONES

BARILOCHE

JACOBACCI

EL BOLSON

ÑORQUINCO

MAITEN

LELEQUE

MADRYN

CHAITEN

ESQUEL

TRELEW

TREVELIN

PUYUHUAPI

PUERTO AISEN

COIHAIQUE

ISLA PAVON

MORENO GLACIER

RIO GALLEGOS

MALVINAS /
FALKLAND ISLANDS

PUNTA ARENAS

For Charlie who took me to Patagonia
and gave me a typewriter.

For our beloved daughters.

For my dear and lovely Argentina.

Chapter One

How I Came To Live
in Patagonia

The house that I grew up in was called Chiru. The Chiruanos were
an indigenous people who occupied that area of the province of Sta
Fé before the influx of European colonists in the second half of the
nineteenth century pushed them north and west towards the mountains. My father liked to tell innocents about the indian chief buried
beneath the front door who wandered the house at night. Pure inven-
tion of course. My grandmother would never have allowed that sort
of thing, nor, for that matter, would my grandfather have killed anyone let alone buried them beneath the front door. The only reminder
of the Chiruanos apart from the name of the house was a square cut
in the ceiling of the room we slept in as children; the remains of a
trap door through which sentries had climbed to keep watch over stock
driven in around the house at night.

It was a long, low house with a verandah and lawns enclosed by
woods of paraiso trees; beyond plains stretched to the horizon.

My grandfather Edmund Traill and his brother Robert were in their
twenties, students of medecine and civil engineering respectively at
Trinity College, Dublin, when they decided, as did so many Irishmen
of their generation, that Ireland, still suffering the effects of the Potatoe
Famine held no future for them. They would emigrate. Within the

British Empire they could find nothing to suit them; Canada was too cold, South Africa too hot and Australia too far. Riffling through the pages of an atlas they came on a name that enchanted them- the Argentine. Argentine, the direct translation of Argentina into English, is a poetic word that also means silvery.

Borrowing from friends and relations they collected five hundred pounds. This was enough to pay their passages to Buenos Aires and leave money over to buy land. When they arrived off the city of Buenos Aires they transferred in the usual way from ship to rowboat to bullock cart to shore. They had decided that they would find the climate they were looking for (climate seems to have mattered more to them than quality of land) on the 33rd parallel which crosses the province of Sta Fé, so they made their way to Rosario where they picked out on a map and bought five leagues of land for which they paid two hundred pesos the league.

From Rosario they took the river boat to Coronda arriving there, probably, at the end of 1869. Their mood must surely have matched the bright patches of ceibo in flower on the banks of the Parana. What were the discomforts of a dirty, little river boat or the attacks of voracious Sta Fé mosquitos to two vigorous, self reliant young men with five leagues of virgin pampa awaiting them? In the only photographs I have seen of them their walrus moustaches are already white, but the air of self confidence is as unmistakable as the powerful torsos that many of their sons inherited.

Coronda is on the Paraná sixteen leagues east of the block of land the brothers had bought. They got in touch with the provincial surveyor, bought a cart and horses, hired a man and a boy and set out westwards. The first few leagues were already staked out, the rest of the way had to be chained through scrub and ant hills, swamp and pasto puna. When they reached their destination and the surveyor had

2

marked the limits of their land their first job was to make themselves a hut with the branches of scrub trees and plaster it with mud.

When I knew it, some fifty years later, only isolated specimens of the original vegetation remained on that flat, flat stretch of pampa. In the 1860's it must have been thickly scattered with small leaved, prickly trees, algarobo, sina sina, espinillo..... The bird life, still abundant fifty years later must then have been almost overpowering. Martineta, good eating and slow off the ground, the first species to disappear as the plains were settled, partridges exploding from beneath a horses' hooves, glossy black tordos, clownish pirinchos and playful calandrias. Terus screamed, bicho feos shouted, chimangos and caranchos floated overhead on the look out for carrion, burrowing owls swivelled their heads to watch them pass and clouds of little birds formed, dissolved and formed again.

All one can be sure of regarding those first years is that they were usually uncomfortable, often boring and sometimes dangerous. Edmund's medical training came in useful. He called his house Chirú, Robert's, ten kilometres further south, was called Las Limpias. They had some trouble with indians and rustlers but the indian frontier where lonely estancias had watch towers and moats and needed them, ran further west. A bigger threat to the Traill brothers would have been the armies that battled back and forth in would have been the armies that battled back and forth in those disturbed times requisitioning cattle, horses and men.

The brothers were fortunate in the time of their arrival in Argentina. Cows which had cost them as little as $0.80 or $1.00 each in 1870 went up steadily in value, and so did land. Surplus animals were trooped some two hundred kilometres to Rosario twice a year —more often if the shortage of cash was acute- and sold for their skins at a peso to a peso fifty apiece to the 'saladero' on a buff above the river.

As soon as they could afford to do so Robert and Edmund imported bulls and stallions to improve their stock. This paid off once cattle began to be valued for meat and not just hide; rather earlier in the case of horse stock. Like most of the inhabitants of the pampas in those days they were very keen on 'cuadreras', the criollo style of horse racing where two compete at a time and there are numerous false starts as the jockeys struggle for an advantage. There was a shortage of ready cash and bets were not always redeemed in money. The handsome oak sideboard that stood in the dining room at Chirú was, I believe, won on a horse race.

After twenty years Robert and Edmund owned twenty two leagues of land. They had made their fortunes in Argentina but their minds and hearts remained in the British Isles. They spent more time and money retiring to live as country gentlemen in England, educating their sons at public school and university, than in looking after the source of their wealth. So they nearly lost it.

In the Baring Crisis of the eighteen nineties the Traill brothers lost three quarters of their property. The value of the paper peso against gold dropped suddenly; the Traills assets were in paper, their debts in gold Edmund left the Manor House at Long Stratton in Norfolk and returned to Argentina with his young wife and family to live in Chirú, then a little, square house at the centre of a circle of treeless plain. My father used to tell us that the best bull was removed from the room that was we knew as the drawing room in preparation for my grandmother's arrival. For the last lap of their journey the family were given a lift in a wagon hooked onto the back of a ballast train, courtesy of the British railways that were spreading across the country.

Edmund had married late. Joe, his eldest son was three years old at the time of the Baring Crisis. He had tutors and governesses, when

4

available as he grew up and plenty of books to read. The sort of education that W.H. Hudson describes in Far Away and Long Ago. When he was seventeen he was left in charge of Chirú while his father and mother took the four younger children to England to be educated.

My grandmother, the daughter of a clergyman, was English. She was a person of character and culture, anxious for her children reared in that rough, frontier style, and instilled in them a horror of alcohol and a high idea of what they owed the world as Englishmen—though they were indeed half Irish.

After the Baring Crisis the situation of the farmer in Argentina gradually improved. A landowner after the turn of the century had time to spare. My father spent his playing polo to a nine handicap, tennis, cricket, billiards, chess, poker and any other game that came his way. It was while playing polo in Ireland that he met the lively Dublin girl who became his wife. The rest of the family, three brothers and a sister, lived in England. Two of the boys, one of whom died in the first World War, became doctors. The youngest joined the Royal Airforce, the Royal Flying Corps it was then called, and retired as Air Vice Marshall after the Second World War.

The only girl, Agnes, married a doctor who shared a practice with her brother and another doctor in Devon. They lived in a rambling farm house and here, among the tiny fields, the banks and beeches of south Devon we stayed when in 1949 my father took his wife and three youngest daughters to England on a visit. It was my mother and father's first since the end of the Second World War which had passed like a hurricane over the Argentine branch of the Traill family taking with it sons, cousins, husbands, brothers. The last time I had stayed with Uncle Frank and Auntie Agnes was during the war when the lawns had been ploughed up and sown with broad beans and potatoes. The house had sheltered a changing population of wives and babies evacuated from cities targeted by German bombers, Argentine volunteers on leave and anyone else in need of a home. It was a sometimes troublesome household kept in order by Auntie Agnes who combined a compassionate heart with a firm hand and a gift for organisation.

Her husband, Frank, was a delightful man. It must have been tiring to have the house filled with his wife's relations for weeks on end and attend to his practice at the same time, but this was never allowed to appear. The time and effort my father put into running his brother's and sisters's share of Chirú estancia, the food parcels that had been posted to them every month through the British Council in Argentina during the war and afterwards, were never forgotten.

All the family were called in to help satisfy my father's appetite for golf, poker and bridge. Invitation after invitation for a return visit to Argentina was refused. Uncle Frank's joy was fly fishing, any time he could spare from his practice was spent by some river in Scotland or Ireland. Then, while we were there, a friend from Argentina dropped in for a meal. When the subject of fishing came up she sang the praises of the fishing in southern Argentina. That same evening to my father's delight and bewilderment –to him a fish was just a food and not a favourite one- Uncle Frank agreed to come to Chirú.

The visit was arranged for December of that same year. My father got to work with his usual energy hiring a car and a driver and preparing a strenuous programme of poker, bridge and barbeques to keep his sister and her husband amused until the day in early January 1950 when Uncle Frank, Auntie Agnes, myself as interpreter and Avelino, the owner driver of the car, set out southwards towards the streams and rivers of northern Patagonia.

We drove for three days; first across the plains of Sta Fé and Buenos Aires to Bahia Blanca then south and west towards the Andes. As Uncle Frank's excitement grew we spent less and less time on meals and stops.

Auntie Agnes' stoical endurance became mutiny when, on the last day of the drive, we rose early from uncomfortable beds in a bad hotel and travelled breakfastless past a chain of towns set back off the road so as not to waste time driving into them. Uncle Frank had a stomach ulcer, and needed to eat at regular intervals. The Rio Negro valley was not set up for travellers in 1950. We stopped at last for a drink of watery coffee and some stale biscuits at a wretched roadside fonda. It was just as well that we did. After that there was nothing in the way of human habitation until a tiny collection of houses called Piedra del Aguila nearly two hundred kilometres further on.

After Piedra del Aguila, where we lunched, the road became two wheel tracks, unfenced and unsigned, that wandered up and down over rolling hills, gradually rising as we approached the Andes. Avelino chose by instinct the set of tracks to follow when occasionally another set joined in. Thanks to his intuition we arrived that evening at a comfortable fishing lodge, a group of cabins between a poplar lined road and the river Limay.

Auntie Agnes and I were sitting out of doors enjoying the sun and the stillness next morning, when Uncle Frank appeared looking as near as possible sulky. Directly after breakfast he had prepared a rod and gone off to the riverside. Avelino accompanied him; he liked fishing, he said, he had once spent a day on a lake outside Cordoba city and enjoyed it very much. Uncle Frank hooked two good fish at a place where it was impossible to land them without a net. Both had got away because Avelino, instead of bringing the net up from underneath, had poked down from above. With no language in common there was nothing that Uncle Frank could do. The fish he landed at a spot where no net was required consoled him not at all at that moment, for the two he had lost. Not many others escaped him.

That afternoon I went for a stroll. As I bent down to get between the wires of a fence a small snake slithered away from under my foot, not something I expected to see in Patagonia and never have since. I crossed the pebbly edge of a stream to a rock that stood in the water. Sitting on that sun warmed rock with the bubbling voices of the stream in my ears I experienced one of the two moments in my life when I have felt the touch of something outside normal, human reality. By the time I walked back to the fishing lodge I knew beyond a doubt that my life lay among country things. Cities and streets were not for me.

It was a memorable trip. We all enjoyed ourselves though fishing did not appeal to me. Uncle Frank caught numbers of rainbow trout and 'trucha criolla' a fish of the perch family native to the Andes, as well as the only salmon caught that season in the Paso Flores fishing lodge. Auntie Agnes did well in her less single minded way. I fell in love with Patagonia and with the Australian manager of a sheep farm through which Uncle Frank's favourite river, the Caleufu, ran.

Charlie was just over thirty, tall, good looking and extremely shy, especially with women. Life on lonely sheep farms does not make for ease of communication. He lived in Alicura, a low house sheltered by Lombardy poplars as were all homesteads in that part of Patagonia. Hollyhocks grew along a white paling fence that edged the lawn infront of the house.

When after three weeks we turned our back on the mountains and headed home to Chirú Uncle Frank said,

"I'd like to think of you as the lady of Alicura."

I was never that. By the time Charlie and I married, four years later, he had taken a step up in The Argentine Southern Land Company for which he worked and was managing another of their properties.

Chapter Two

The Argentine Southern
Land Company

In 1935 Charlie was eighteen and had finished his education at Geelong College and Longernon Agricultural College in Australia. His one wish was to work on the land. As he found it difficult to find a job in Australia which was still affected by the Depression, he wrote to his uncle, Bill Mackinnon, the General Manager of the Argentine Southern Land Company, to ask for work. Charlie's father had died when he was a child, Bill Mackinnon , unknown to Charlie then and for years later, had paid the expenses of his education. It was particularly appropriate that he should have written to him.

The Argentine Southern Land Company, referred to in written reports as the ASL and known within the spheres of influence of its various properties as La Compania or The Company, was formed in the 1890's with British capital to buy land in Southern Argentina after General Roca in The Conquest of the Desert Campaign of 1880 to 1883 had opened up Argentina south of the Rio Negro to settlement. Generous terms were offered by the Argentine government to attract settlers and investment. Walter Woodbine Parish, one time British Consul in Argentina, recognised the opportunity; his name is connected with the purchase.

Before General Roca's campaign Argentina ended on the Indian frontier that cut across the province of Buenos Aires. Over half the country's total length from north to south was controlled by indigenous tribes; south of Bahia Blanca, apart from two or three enclaves of European settlement on the coast and a missionary station on Tierra del Fuego, it was Indian country.

The Argentine government tried to conciliate the caciques with gifts of horses, money and rations, but periods of peaceful co-existence never lasted. Raiding parties would cross the line of 'fortines' made at intervals along a sort of moat to try and keep them out of the settled areas of the province of Buenos Aires, sweeping back with herds of cattle and horses; sometimes with women and children. The Indians drove the cattle across the continent and sold them for a good price in Chile.

The Argentine Southern Land Company pioneered the empty spaces that had been opened up. The first managers travelled for days across trackless country on horseback or in horse drawn vehicles. I remember a sentence from Company correspondence in those early years. One of the managers had not been heard of for months. 'Patagonia is a bad place to be ill,' writes a director sombrely.

Rations, posts and building materials were brought by ship to ports on the Atlantic coast and then overland by mule train. Over the years the years the land was surveyed and fenced. Before that it might be noted down in the diary kept by every estancia manager, that the horse boy had gone to fetch a troop of riding horses. Ten days, a fortnight or three weeks later, perhaps, it would be noted down that he had returned, with or without the horses.

The homesteads were islands of civilisation. The facilities the Company developed over the years were used by national as well as private organisations and individuals. The army putting up telegraph wires, the police in their double function as the arm of the law and succour to people in difficulties, road and railway makers looked to the Company for help and co-operation over the decades.

Married men were not employed until sometime in the 1920's and even then women were tolerated rather than encouraged. I remember a wife who was still annoyed by this thirty years later, but I find the directors' attitude understandable. It was difficult for a woman from a middle class background in the British Isles to adapt to the loneliness, the lack of social life and of the company of women of her own kind. Few of them learned to speak Spanish.

Some could take it. Others had affairs with the men who surrounded them, became dependent on alcohol, unbalanced in one way or another. One manager's wife was snobbish to a degree that was ridiculous , laughable, if one did not have to live on the same homestead with her, extremely irritating if one did. It was not until Uncle Bill happened to mention being asked to read the funeral service over the grave of a child of hers that I saw it as a rather pathetic sort of defence —one not uncommon among British expatriates in the days of Empire.

The Argentine Southern Land Company was part of the history of Patagonia —northern Patagonia. The northern boundary of Patagonia is commonly taken to be the River Colorado. Those who live around the southern tip of South America, in Rio Gallegos for instance, or on the Island of Tierra del Fuego where winter lasts from April to November and the sun hardly clears the horizon in the darkest months, find it rather ridiculous that the inhabitants of the provinces of Chubut, Rio Negro and Neuquen call themselves Patagonians. The northern boundary of the Province of Chubut which runs through Maiten estancia of which Charlie was manager when we married, is the 42nd parrallel.

When I first knew it the Company owned about 500.000 hectares of land. It had become something of a legend: politicians and journalists exaggerated, for their own purposes, the size of the properties and the number of sheep they carried. Once at a political rally in Luna

Park we heard one of the speakers say that he had been told in Esquel that all the land between that town and Bariloche was owned by an English company that produced some incredible number of kilos of wool annually on this tremendous property. The distance between the two places as the crow flies is about the same as the distance between the north and southern boundaries of the province of Tucuman. Tucuman has an area of just over two and a quarter million hectares. The only English company owning land between Esquel and Bariloche was The Argentine Southern Land and the total area of the three properties it owned north of Esquel and south of Bariloche was about four hundred thousand hectares. The excellence of the stock they carried attracted as much envy as admiration, as though good stock was the result of a happy accident rather than hard work and clever management.

The four Southern Land properties in the pre-Cordillera were, from south to north and biggest to smallest, Leleque, Maiten, Pilcaneu and Alicura. There was another property in central Patagonia and one in the province of Buenos Aires was rented early on for fattening surplus stock from the southern estancias. Later it was run as a separate entity.

The Company was run from River Plate House, Finsbury Circus, London, by a board of directors. Directors and Boards of directors meant nothing to me until I married Charlie. In the Company they mattered. His long relationship with his bosses was one of affection and respect on both sides, tempered by the usual human rubs between bosses and the bossed.

Charlie was in charge of the Montoso section of Leleque in September 1939. When he heard on his radio that war had been declared on Germany by the British Commonwealth he rode into the main homestead to tell the manager that he was leaving to join up. The journey to Australia was too expensive for a trainee on a low salary so he volunteered for the British Army. Passages for volunteers for the British Armed forces were paid from Buenos Aires to the United Kingdom.

He joined a cavalry regiment, the Scots Greys, because he loved and understood horses. They were converted almost immediately to tanks. Taking part in a jumping competition before this happened he did a bad round. Annoyed at not being able to communicate with his mount he took off the bulky army saddle, jumped on and did a clear round bareback. His superiors were not pleased; he'd got his priorities wrong.

The Scots Greys trained in freezing conditions in the north of Scotland —presumably a Scandinavian campaign was contemplated- and ended up in Africa. During a military exercise in Scotland it poured with rain the whole two days. Confusion reigned. Wet, lost and hungry Charlie was walking along a village street when he passed a group of high ranking officers.

"What's wrong corporal?" one of them called out.

Charlie explained that he had lost his unit.

"Dont let that worry you," said the officer, a General Ritchie, "I lost an army in Africa."

Charlie took part in the battles of Torbruk, Alamein and Monte Casino and carried on up the length of Italy. The end of the war found him in Udine near the frontier with Switzerland.

After so much of death and destruction, the iron routine of army life, like so many volunteers to the Armed Forces he found it difficult to get back to civilian attitudes; the rythm of life on a Patagonian estancia.

Chapter Three

Maiten Estancia

We were married on August 5th 1954 in Buenos Aires and travelled south a week or two later by train. Early on the second morning, at the station of Jaccobacci in the high, cold centre of Patagonia, we changed onto the narrow guage railway that runs south and westwards to the terminal in the town of Esquel.

All that day the trencito, as it was called, twisted and turned among barren looking hills, sometimes turning back on itself like a worm. After leaving Ñorquinco, the last station before our destination, El Maiten, it passed on an embankment above a shallow lagoon through a gap into a wide, flat bottomed valley, the valley of the river Chubut. It was walled to the west by snow topped mountains, their slopes darkened where the snow ended by forests of leafless trees.

Another three quarters of an hour and the trencito stopped in El Maiten, fifteen minutes drive from the homestead of Maiten Estancia of which Charlie was manager. Even the lower hills were patched with snow on that bleak, late winter afternoon. A fire in the drawing room and an iced cake on a table set for tea made a cheerful contrast with out-of-doors. Dina and Argentino, who looked after the house for Charlie had laid themselves out to provide a warm welcome.

The homestead stood in the valley of the Chubut between the river and the range that closed it to the east. The windows at the front of the house looked over a lawn, trees and a tennis court, long out of use, to a row of reddish cliffs and a square, black gloomy looking rock on the skyline. Between the homestead and the range was a road, the ruta cuarenta that runs along the Argentine side of the Andes from the frontier with Bolivia to about a hundred kilometres from the Straits of Magellan. Beyond the road, about a kilometre from the homestead, ran the railway. If the ground was wet a passing train made the windows rattle. At the back of the house rows of Lombardy poplars swayed and rustled and thundered in the westerly winds .

The western side of the Chubut valley was formed by the first ranges of the Andes proper, always referred to as the Cordillera. Everything to do with the weather, and weather is the most important element in farm life, seemed to come from the Cordillera. The mountains were much more than a merely physical presence to those who lived at their feet.

"The Cordillera is looking angry" the gardener might say, meaning that bad weather was on the way.

When eating an asado I was advised always to sit with my back to the Cordillera to avoid getting smoke in my eyes. One of the men on the estancia remarked that no good would come of this business of aeroplanes flying back and forth across the mountains; it would anger them. Sometimes when the sky overhead was blue flakes of snow or drops of rain reached us on the wind.

The house itself had once been a shearing shed. A passage with rooms on either side ran from the offices at one end to the front door at the other. The ceilings were lofty, the rooms large and bright. Like most of the managers' houses on the Company properties it had been changed about and added on to over the years. The kitchen was rather dark and the wooden floor of the wide verandah that ran the length and width of the house was difficult to keep clean, but it was a comfortable house to live in if not an easy one to run.

There was an endearing lack of pretentiousness about all the managers' houses in the Company but one. This was due to the fact that most of them had grown up over the years, that the managers were their own architects and that the directors looked after the stockholders' money very carefully. Nothing was done merely for show.

Salaries were kept up to date, not such a common virtue in rural Patagonia, but they were not very generous. As a result of laws brought in during Peron's time the salaries of the lower ranges of workers employed by the Company, labourers, shepherds, foremen, mechanics, were improved, as were their living conditions. As a foreign company the Argentine Southern Land Company paid high taxes and the provincial government made sure it kept within the law.

Managers' salaries were not on a level with their responsibilities and the power they wielded. Schooling was a problem once children got beyond the stage where a governess or the local school was enough. The nearest boarding schools were in Buenos Aires and far too expensive for a manager with no outside source of income. The custom of wives leaving their husbands to live in a town with their children while they were being educated was frowned on in the Company. From being intolerant of women they had learned to appreciate the steadying effect of a wife and family.

When a manager retired he was reduced to a very different level of life; especially if he tried retiring to the England he had dreamed of for years only to find that it no longer existed, or was accessible only to people far better off. Some were reduced to actual poverty. Until Peron introduced them there were no laws regarding pensions.

The Company was full of traditions and hierachies. One odd custom was re-naming camp assistants, young men starting off with the Company. The administrative staff were known by their christian names, Don Juan say, or Don Francisco. New Camp assistants were re-named if their names were unpronounceable in Spanish –Alistair for instance- or if they happened to be working for a senior member of the staff who had the same name. Once named there was no changing it for the duration of a man's time in the Company. Thus Charlie, Charles William Mackinnon, was Don Guillermo though Charles transelates into Spanish as Carlos; his Uncle Bill was Don Carlos though William transelates as Guillermo. It made for confusion when the outer world impinged on Company life.

As I have said before, in the Company the Directors, there were usually four or five, mattered. Some of them bore names that are part of the history of the development of Argentina into a great farming nation; Waldron, Wood, Carlisle. At least once a year a Director, usually accompanied by his wife, made a tour of inspection staying several days on each property; occasionally several came together. We manager's wives entertained them to the best of our varying resources and abilities. I found them undemanding and easy to get on with though it was a strain to raise our style of life to the level one imagined they expected. It took me a few years to realise that simplicity, friendliness and privacy were what they most appreciated on a journey of several weeks changing households every few days.

I never remember being allowed to feel that our hospitality was lacking. I cannot remember so much as a reproachful look except on two occasions, which says a lot for the restraint and good manners of our directors. The first was when a director came on his own and I had forgotten to make sure that the roll of toilette paper in his bathroom had been renewed.

The second was equally well deserved. In my own home the food at meals had never been handed. My father at one end of the table carved, then the plates were passed down to the other where my mother helped the vegetables. This system was perfectly adequate among family and friends but it seemed awkward putting the directors to work and, besides, it interrupted the conversation. I decided to have the vegetables handed. This plan, a good one as a plan, depended as I did not realise on a supply of trained help accustomed to that way of doing things. Elena was an intelligent girl but we had not practised enough. The second reproachful look came when a roast potatoe rolled into a silken lap —we always dressed for dinner when the directors were with us- from a dish held not quite level.

The ceremonial that surrounded director's visits was a carry over from the days when they came by ship from England to Puerto Madryn or Trelew on the Atlantic coast and drove across the country in horse drawn vehicles. Then their stay on each of the properties might last a month and served to bring managers up to the mark; correct any care-lessness that might have crept into their way of living.

I sometimes remembered what I had read about the East India Company as I learned about the Argentine Southern Land Company. The manager of each of the properties was a power in the district around even in my late day when the railway, roads and telegraph lines had broken the isolation and there was an infrastructure of police, doctors and municipalities holding society together.

Chapter Four

Living and Learning

The town was called El Maiten and the estancia Maiten, without the article. The maiten (maitenus boaria) is a tree, a stately evergreen with hanging foliage and small, dancing leaves. I do not remember maiten trees round the town and only one or two small ones on the homestead, but there may have been before settlers cut them down. The logs burn well, throwing out more heat and lasting longer that most other woods.

In that latitude the western or Chilean side of the Andes is thickly forested. The eastern, Argentine, slopes are wooded though not so thickly and the foothills are bare except for trees that mark the line of watercourses. As the rainfall diminishes the farther east one goes so does the plant life. The prickly neneo bushes and clumps of tussock grass that cover and hold the stoney hill-sides in place in the pre-Cordillera, become more and more dispersed, until on the Atlantic coast the bushes are spaced and the tussock is gone.

When I arrived in Patagonia I felt that I had stepped back to an earlier Argentina. The big store-room at Chirú, built for my grandmother in the days when a bullock cart set off on a three day journey twice a month to get rations and the mail, had been converted into two good sized bathrooms in the thirties. By then my mother did her shopping in the near by town. On the Company properties there was no lack of bathrooms but pioneering days were much closer when it came to rations.

In the little Wild West town of El Maiten fresh foods were only occasionally available. We were dependent on what the estancia produced for milk, eggs, vegetables and, of course, beef and mutton. I do not mention fruit because the homestead was about 700 metres above sea level and though there were cherry and apple trees, even a quince, they rarely produced fruit.

I was allowed two people to help me in the house and a gardener for outside. Dina cooked and Argentino cleaned; they had two small children. Good natured, untidy Dina, a good cook when she felt like it, was the first of many women and girls to work for me. Argentino was the only man I ever had working in the house. I felt very proud of him when he waited at table in his white coat, always spotless and efficient.

They left a few years later when he was offered a job in the railway workshops in El Maiten. Dina had a way with animals. Her black cat, Negro, who always lay on the top shelf of the dresser in the kitchen went with them. When he found that he had to share a crowded house with other dogs and cats he found his way across the fields to his old home. Dina gave him to our eldest daughter, Moira, and he became part of the Mackinnon family; the wisest, most family minded cat that I have ever known.

The girls who came to cook and clean were all either wholly or partly indian. Paisano was the word we used when we referred to the desendants of the indigenous tribes, usually Araucano or Tehuelche in that part of Argentina. Most of them had some European blood. The word 'paisano' can mean either fellow countryman or peasant. Among people who think that European blood is in some way superior it carries a touch of denigration. Not as I use it.

20

Most of the girls who came to work for me were from the town of El Maiten; many from the poor quarter where wooden shacks lined streets only just wide enough to take a car that led down to the river Chubut. A few came from the very lowest levels of poverty. They would arrive dirty in clothes and person and become clean overnight. I remember one in particular with as pretty face and the mis-shapen legs that are the result of malnutrition in childhood.

They kept their hair, uniforms and persons spotless. Of an afternoon they would light a fire beneath the petrol drum that did duty as a tank in the wash house, and in the iron box used for heating flat irons. With a kettle of water for mate they would wash, iron and drink mate to their heart's content.

The pleasure of having plenty of food, hot water and money to spend soon wore off. The regular working hours got the girls down and after a few months, perhaps a year, they would disappear, usually without giving notice, into the comfortably unregulated poverty from which they had come.

Maiten was the worst property I lived on for the coming and going of domestic staff. This was due mostly to the attractions of the town close by, but also because I did not understand them. For thousands of years their ancestors had wandered Patagonia without calendars or clocks, living each day as it came, measuring time by the rising and setting of the sun and by the seasons, feasting when there was food, going without when there was none. They could not adapt to our European way of life where time was measured in hours and minutes.

When I had learned more about life in Patagonia I gave the girls who came to work for me a talk. First I told them that we lived on a homestead where there were twenty men to each woman and not to believe all they were promised.

"Most men are looking for one thing and be careful how you give

21

it or you will find yourself with a baby and no one to help you support it."

I would have expected this advice to be unnecessary but it was effective. Marriage was not common even among couples who had lived together for years until, sometime in the sixties, laws were introduced giving monetary benefits for each child of married couples. Fine old paisano women, very much the head of the family group, looked after their children and their children's children in company cottages out on the lonely, rolling hills.

The second point I made was that there were two sides to our contract. It I found their work unsatisfactory I would either give them time to find another job or an extra month's salary. If they wanted to leave they must give me time to find a replacement.

Most of these girls had musical names. Some were incorrect versions of names; in those days in lonely areas, the Juez de Paz with whom births were registered, might be only slightly more instructed than his neighbours. Lauriana, Aldina, Pola, Aidalida, Dalia, the list ripples on. It was pleasant to get away from Rosa, Maria and Elena.

We were allowed a gardener to cut lawns and hedges, feed the hens, do odd jobs and, most important of all, look after the vegetable garden. It was easy to find men and boys to do the other jobs – vegetables were the problem. Unlike the Italians who settled the country round Chirú the Indians of southern Argentina had no tradition of working the soil. In their natural state they had eaten what nature provided. A few roots and berries and some medicinal herbs were all that varied their diet of ostrich and guanaco meat. There was no place in their lives for digging and sowing. A man might tame a horse in his spare time but never tend a garden. I think the gardeners, especially the younger ones, came in for some heavy teasing in the bunk house. Real men worked in the sheep corrals and on horseback.

Cruz, the gardener I found when I arrived in Maiten estancia, was exceptional in two aspects; he could read and write well and he knew quite a lot about about growing vegetables. Both these accomplishments he had acquired in prison to which he was sent for killing his wife when he found her with another man.

After years of bachelor managers who had left him to do pretty much as he liked it must have been tiresome to have a woman in charge - even one who knew nothing about growing vegetables. He was a dear old man though he didn't work very hard; he was too old for it. One afternoon I came on him and the boy he had been given to help him, sitting in the sunshine with their backs up against the box in which the garden implements were kept, sound asleep.

The second essential on an estancia was a well run hen run. Our hen run had been neglected for years though there were indications that at one time it had been well looked after. A German couple who, after years of efficient service, had been told to leave when the Second World War broke out, were the last to have reared chickens there in numbers.

I knew as little about hens as I did about vegetables. For some months I made it my business to ask any woman I met, Dina, the wives of shopkeepers in El Maiten, of foremen and managers, how they ran their hen runs, collecting a mass of miscellaneous information, some of it contradictory, from which I did not know enough to pick out the true from the false.

On one occasion I spent the greater part of a wedding supper, at which I found myself seated next to the man in charge of a section of Leleque estancia, discussing hens. I remember his remarking that black hens make the best mothers. How right he was! To this day I remember with affection that little black hen, the first I ever set. This sensible and intelligent fowl went off to eat and drink each day when I picked her off her eggs, had a satisfying dust bath and then settled back on the nest. She brought out twelve chicks from fourteen eggs. I never did better than that and usually much worse.

Hysterical hens that started up screaming when I came near, irresponsible hens that stayed off the nest too long and let the eggs grow cold, dopey hens that would settle down on a nest with no eggs in it while their own grew cold in the one next door, I got to know them all. The walk to the hen run along a row of poplars roaring in the spring gales grew very familiar.

Though the river Chubut ran a few hundred metres from the homestead its waters had not been put to use. The problem was to raise them. At one point a water wheel made years before stood on the bank; changes in the water level had left the canal that fed it dry. In the first year of our marriage Charlie worked out a system whereby the level of the water in the river was raised by a low dam higher up the valley and brought five kilometres to the homestead by scraping out a channel where the lie of the land was not favourable. Then there was no shortage of water to irrigate pine plantations, fields of alfalfa, the vegetable garden and the lawn.

Charlie persuaded the directors to have modern lavatories made for the bunk house in place of the outhouse variety. The men did not understand or approve of the new system. The lavatories were stopped up by rubbish thrown down them, men were seen riding into town with rolls of toilet paper on sticks like flags unwinding.

Charlie called the men together. Goodness knows what he said to them in his forceful, expressive, Australian paisano dialect. Somebody laughed. Charlie lost his temper; it was a subject that meant a great deal to him.

"Who laughed?" he cried, dancing round in an undignified way with his fists raised. "Laugh again. Just laugh again —"

Nobody laughed but it was still many months before modern hygiene caught on in Maiten bunk house.

The usual form of entertaining in the Company was an asado. A lamb or half a sheep or, in the winter months when we ate beef, part of a steer (whose butchering was probably the reason for the asado) was speared on an iron stake and leaned over the fire to cook. Sausages, kidneys and other innards cooked on a grill over coals drawn from the fire began the meal.

When the main roast was ready bread was sliced and each person, a slice of bread in one hand a knife in the other, cut off the piece they fancied. The meat was held on the bread with a thumb while cutting off mouthfuls, taking each piece between the teeth as the last strands were cut. Most people brought their own, well sharpened knives. It took a little time to learn to eat neatly – the directors never attempted it, a table was set for them – but it was worth it. Meat, especially mutton or lamb, is neither so hot nor so tasty eaten off a plate. As we chatted round the fire waiting for the meat to cook the mate passed from hand to hand; some drank wine poured from a demijohn.

When I had been in Maiten for a year or so Charlie decided that we should have an asado for neighbours and local authorities to whom the estancia owed favours. An advantage of asados from a woman's point of view is that the main part of the meal is not her responsibility. We in the kitchen concentrated on salads and desserts.

I learned on this occasion that to invite people to a midday asado in Patagonia was to invite them to tea, sometimes to supper as well. When at six o'clock our guests were still sitting on the verandah gazing dreamily out across the lawn, over the hawthorne trees to the red cliffs and the black rock above, I realised that something must be prepared for tea. In Patagonia guests are slow to leave when they are enjoying themselves but undemanding with it.

Another thing I noticed in the Company was the lack of any sport. Coming from a family of compulsive sportsmen and women it seemed strange just to sit on after an asado instead of playing,or improvising, a game. One wet week end at Chirú when the house was full we played a tennis tournament on the verandah using folded deck chairs propped on their sides as a net.

Our classic entertainment after a big asado was a game we called hoc-po-ten (hockey, polo, tennis). Everyone found themselves some sort of implement, a worn out broom, a polo stick cut down, a twisted branch, an old raquet or even, if they were in the know, a proper hockey stick, and we played hockey with a polo ball on the lawn infront of the house. If one couldn't get the ball by fair means one got it by foul; the more energetic ran up and down, the less so took it easy. The afternoon passed on with fun and energy loosed off.

This did not happen at asados in the Company. There was no tradition of sport. All the bigger properties had tennis courts but most had gone to seed. Unless someone organised a walk or a climb, a tug of war or a gambling game people just sat around talking and drank more wine than was good for them.

Chapter Five

Early Years

Our three daughters Moira, Joan and Flora, were all born while Charlie was managing Maiten. Moira was just on five years old, Joan four and Flora one when, in 1960, we went to live in Leleque. Big houses, plenty of space, earth and grass, trees to climb and animals for company, there is no better place for rearing children than a farm. The eternal presence of demanding little beings, the most exhausting part of bringing up children, was reduced -though it was a daily relief when the office door opened and the children rushed down the passage to pile themselves on their father.

From the point of view of medical attention, however, rearing children on a farm in Patagonia was not ideal. We were lucky to have an excellent doctor within reach. I will never forget the first time I went to see Dr Manz. I had lost faith in the doctor in El Maiten. Antibiotics were beginning to be in general use. For the sore throats all our children suffered, especially in spring, he would prescribe an antibiotic. The throat cleared up then in a week or two became inflamed again ..... more antibiotics.

I spoke to Charlie about it and the next time one of the children needed medical attention he drove us northwards up the Chubut valley, through the gap the train came through, to the tiny, desolate town of Ñorquinco. We drove past an irregular line of shacks before turning off the road on to a track that lead to a little house that seemed part of the hill it backed onto. The wooden door was closed with a heavy latch like the one on a stable door. It was a relief to be shown off an earth floored indoor patio full of plants, into a consulting room that was bright and clean, if as bare and poor as the rest of the establishment. The doctor himself set all doubts to rest. He had a massive head, white hair, a keen youthful expression and seemed too big for his consulting room. Perhaps the confidence he exuded made him seem bigger than he was. With only the most primitive aids he was an excellent diagnostician and, as he always knew exactly what he was dealing with, would cure with an aspirin ills for which lesser doctors prescribed atibiotics. I never knew him wrong and I sent many people to him.

He had taken his degree in Germany. As he never renewed it in Argentina he was driven out of the more prosperous areas when an Argentine medical degree became obligatory. He had attended Company personnel until the same foolish directive that had deprived Maiten estancia of the excellent German couple who ran the staff house, deprived it too of the services of the best doctor in the area.

No one envied him Ñorquinco where his practice consisted mainly of Indians from the Cushamen area which was reserved for them. When I had undressed our little daughter and she lay on the couch he looked at her for a moment before he began his examination. The tragic implications of his next remark have kept them fresh in my memory.

"How pleasant it is," he observed, "to see a well nourished child."

His wife, a slim, reserved woman, was also German and must also have studied medecine. His eyesight was beginning to fail and he sometimes called her in to confirm a symptom. She loved, she told me, to play the piano. Dr Manz died some years after we left Maiten and is buried in the cemetry in El Maiten. A long column of his patients and friends, some of whom had travelled all day in bullock carts or on horseback to accompany him on his last journey, followed his coffin to the grave.

Every year while our daughters were small I gave a Christmas party sometime in the second half of December, inviting all the smaller children on the homestead. The problem was to find some one to take the part of Father Christmas. Charlie refused the honour very firmly; I needed to be free to organize. I was as surprised as I was pleased when David offered himself for the part.

David was a very young camp assistant. With his round face, innocent manner and crest of unruly hair he looked about eighteen, but I believe he was a year or two older when he came to work in Maiten. I was a bit worried about him when I escaped from the darkened dining room where the guests, mothers and children, were gazing at the lighted Christmas tree with expressions varying from alarm to the stoney look that is the paisanos's typical reaction to something they dont understand.

I found him happily donning the trousers and jacket made up by the cook from some cheap, red material, the cotton wool beard ("Why does Father Christmas have cotton wool on his chin?", one of our daughters asked years later) and the red cap with the pom pom. He wore a pair of the rubber boots issued by the Company to men working in wet conditions with more cotton wool around the tops and Charlie's widest belt. When I told him to stamp along the passage and thump heavily on the door of the dining room to add to the thrill, he agreed cheerfully as if he were enjoying himself.

I cannot say the same of our guests. Looking back I do not wonder. Christmas was not celebrated in those days in the interior of Argentina, except by groups of people descended from northern Europeans, nor was there a tradition of giving toys to children among the paisanos.

We had started off with a rather stiff tea party on the verandah. Few of the six or seven mothers had been in the house before —never as guests- and none was accustomed to drinking tea. The children were affected by their mothers' misgivings. No one ate much and the only ones who talked were Mecha, the estancia book keeper's young wife, recently arrived from Buenos Aires, and myself. After tea I led the party indoors to the dining room where the sun shone obstinately through the curtains, competing with the lights on the Christmas tree.

At the sound of David's footfalls resounding along the passage and his commanding thump on the door some of the smallest children began to cry, all drew nearer to their mothers. He breezed in breathing hale heartiness, rubbing his hands and complaining of the cold; a piece of humour that must have fallen flat on all but Mecha and myself.

He took the sack off his shoulder and, chatting away, began to hand out presents. I think that the only ones that really enjoyed that first Christmas party were David and our children. He took revenge on the naughty boy of the homestead. When he picked up a parcel and called his name the boy stepped forward quickly holding out his hand; naughty boys are seldom timid. David kept hold of the parcel and said with a searching look.

"¿Y tu Enrique, te has portado bien todo el año redondo?"

Enrique prudently made no answer and after a moment of suspense he got his parcel. The next Christmas everything went much more smoothly. Everyone knew what to expect.

That year or the next David fell in love. He was not the sort of person to conceal his feelings and drove Charlie nearly mad one shearing when, instead of attending to his job at the wool classing table, he stood at the door of the shed smiling happily at nothing. The girl was a teacher at the school in El Maiten, a very attractive, practical, intelligent girl of German parentage. He could not have chosen better.

They were married the following winter; the wedding at which I had such an interesting conversation on hens and hen runs with my neighbour at the meal after the ceremony.

Chapter Six

Don Mauricio

The General Manager, the man who, under the direction of the Board of Directors in London, ran the Company, was Don Mauricio. He was kind, straight as a man can be and very shy. He was a New Zealander; by coincidence he shared the same sur-name with Charlie and Uncle Bill, spelt in the same way. I have a feeling that in their usual free and easy way with names in the Company McKinnon or MacKinnon may have been changed to Mackinnon to simplify matters to do with paper work. Foreign names were awkward enough without that sort of thing.

Don Mauricio was a bachelor. It took a whiskey or two to enable him to converse easily with a woman, after another he began to repeat himself –whole stories word for word. For that reason he was not the easiest person to have in the house, but he couldn't have been a better boss or a better person. He drank a good deal, which was understandable in a person who had spent so much of his life on his own, but he was never drunk or offensive.

At a Company celebration an old peón who had worked with him years before might come up to greet him. He would be welcomed with a warm embrace and they would drink and chat together. Next morning Don Mauricio was the boss and no one took any liberties.

He was too old to volunteer for the Second World War and had what I often thought was the hardest part: watching the young men go, keeping up with the fluctuating fortunes of the Allied armies on radio bulletins, reading the lists of the missing and the dead in The Buenos Aires Herald and The Standard, the English language newspapers. When the war ended he celebrated with a super-asado on Leleque estancia of which he was manager at the time. All the countryside was invited to a feast at which every sort of meat from pichi (a sort of armadillo) to ostrich and guanaco meat was provided, as well as the usual mutton and beef. As a matter of fact Don Mauricio, normally careful with Company money, earned himself a rebuke from the Board of Directors on this occasion for overspending.

He had excellent taste in clothes; socks, shoes, coats and ties always perfectly combined and suited to the occasion. If what I heard is true his taste in women was impeccable too. The one he fell in love with and who married his friend was one of the sweetest and best women I have known.

Don Mauricio spent a night or two with us once or twice a month while the roads were open; November to April in a normal year. He lived in the big house (La Casa Grande) on Pilcaneu estancia near the town of Pilcaniyeu, about a hundred kilometres north of Maiten along a lonely road that crossed the watercourses running from the Andes. In those days they were unbridged.

I thought Don Mauricio was at ease with me until, on the last day of one of his visits, Charlie told him that he had to go out early and would not be having breakfast with us next morning. Don Mauricio set out early and did the three hour drive to Pilcaneu without breakfast rather than sit down to a meal alone with me. He did not drive himself and was chauffered by a very decent, respectable man called Ofelio Lopez whom I got to know well after Don Mauricio retired and he came to work in Leleque.

The Big House in Pilcaneu was the exception to the rule of unpretentious houses in the Company. It had been made in about 1920 by a General Manager who was married to a member of a wealthy and well known British family by the name of Guiness. Communications with London were slow; there was no telegraph and letters took about a month. What was an enormous sum of money for the time was spent on the house. By the time the Board realised what was going on all they could do was foot the bill and sack the General Manager. Uncle Bill took over from him.

It was a large, stone built, single story house with a handsome entrance. Everything was of the best quality. In the living part of the house there were five bedrooms, four bathrooms and numerous reception rooms. A wide staircase led up to a roomy attic floor where there were storerooms, another bathroom and a school room. The erring General Manager had had a family of small children and a governess.

The house was a striking sight in that bare landscape. The Pilcaneu homestead was 850 metres above sea level, flowers, plants and trees had to be cosseted, watered and protected from the wind and frost. Uncle Bill had a massive wall built round the back of the house in a not very successful attempt to protect it from the wind.

The reason the previous General Manager went overboard in such a big way (threw the house through the window as the saying is) was, it was said, because the then Prince of Wales, later King Edward VIIIth, was due to visit Argentina in 1926 to open a British Exhibition in Buenos Aires. Later he was to travel on south to San Carlos de Bariloche, the terminal of the Southern Railway. The railways were in British hands and the Southern Railway ran through Pilcaneu property –the reason for its being chosen as the General Manager's head quarters.

The Prince was expected to spend the night in Pilcaneu. I was told by a director that several metres of red carpet had been found in one of the attics; I have myself seen white table clothes with a pattern of rose,thistle and shamrock woven into them, it seems probable that a royal visit was expected.

The Prince did not stay in Pilcaneu. Uncle Bill and some of the staff who waited at Pilcaneu station at some early hour to offer loyal greetings were attended by an Aide de Camp. The Prince was asleep. His brother George came later to spend a day or two.

Don Mauricio lived in a small corner of this great house; it was not easy for him to run it with no wife to help him. Sometimes it was not easy for his guests either. He was very good to the Polish couple who looked after him. I remember one of the directors describing with humour how he and his wife had been given dinner early and sent to bed so as not to keep them up late.

When a general manager retired the other managers took a step up. Don Mauricio retired in 1960 and Charlie was promoted to manage Leleque estancia which shared part of a boundary with Maiten. The homesteads were fifty kilometres apart.

I taught our children to read English when they were four years old, using a series of readers sent to me by a sister who lived in England. I allowed them to read a page a day as a sort of treat, like a chocolate after lunch. They were always wildly curious to see the words and picture on the next page so teaching was painless. When the series finished my sister sent a children's magazine called Playbox. After that they taught themselves.

In the family we always spoke English so it seemed time for Moira to start on the Spanish side of her education. I was determined that our daughters, unlike their father and mother, should speak Spanish correctly and be at home in the culture of the country they lived in.

I was afraid that the two languages might confuse them, but, on the contrary, the English they had learned helped with the Spanish.

In the spring of 1959 Moira started going to school in El Maiten. She brought back and handed on to her sisters first measles, then chicken pox. I spent the greater part of the lovely spring days nursing them. When Flora started with a suspicious whoop I had them all vaccinated against whooping cough and that put an end to that.

It was the year of the Suez Crisis. Charlie was out lamb marking. Lamb marking, one of the mayor operations on a sheep farm, took about ten days on Maiten estancia. For the first five or six, when they were working on the more distant parts of the property, the lamb marking gang camped out. I attended to the children during the day and at night listened to news bulletins on the British Broadcasting radio channel about the mounting crisis. All I could do to relieve the strain was to write to my sister in England telling her not to hesitate to send her children to me should it come to war. The crisis was well past by the time I got her answer saying she always intended, if worst came to worst, to sent them out to the family in Argentina. The wife of the British Prime Minister, Mrs Eden, said at the time that she felt as if the Suez Canal was running through her drawing room. A drop or two splashed down in Patagonia.

When a general manager retired he was given a farewell party in Pilcaneu. Traditionally this and the change over of managers took place in July, midwinter, the quietest time of the year as far as work, or indeed anything else, was concerned. Pilcaneu was the highest and coldest of the properties.

A Company party was unusual and great fun engendering the sort of warmth that people who do not meet often and have many interests in common, create. We collected in the Big House, the staff and manager's houses in Pilcaneu on a Saturday and there was a party that night. Next morning we rose late and gathered in one of the sheds well after midday for drinks and an asado. There was a delicious looking cake of the kind known as mil hojas for dessert.

We were about half way through the asado and the fun inside the shed was fast and furious when Charlie came up to me and said,

"I've been talking to Montenegro. He says it is going to snow. We'd better get home. I'll take you up to the house to pack while I get the car ready." Montenegro was a very experienced old foreman.

Everyone tried to persuade us to stay on, at least until after the meal, but then no one else had small children with them. As we drove away the rest of the party were standing at the entrance to the shed laughing and waving, glass in hand. I did regret that cake.

As we drove home across the grey hills we saw cattle and horses standing with their tails to the wind, a sure sign of a 'temporal', a period of bad weather. By the time we reached Maiten it was starting to snow. No one else got away from Pilcaneu for a week and then only as far as Bariloche, an hour's drive away. After a week Don Mauricio was tired of having managers hanging around doing nothing to earn their keep.

"Of course the roads are dry! Everything has dried out"
he'd say, we were told, pressing his foot into the ground and drawing it out with a squelch.

It was good to get back to Maiten after that wintry drive and find the house warm, fires burning in the rooms and Aldina at the door with a welcoming smile. Aldina was the most intelligent of the girls who worked for me in my 26 years in the Company.

Her father had died when she was a child, leaving her mother in abject poverty. When I knew her first Aldina lived in a shepherds's cottage behind the range infront of Maiten homestead. She was eighteen when she came to work for us some six months before we made the change to Leleque. She had no schooling, knew nothing about cleaning or cooking and was so innocent that when the departing cook, a malicious woman, told her to shake hands with the guests before handing round the coffee she did so, to our surprise and that of the friends who had lunched with us.

She left us eight years later to marry a member of the fencing gang in Leleque and become the staff house cook. By then she had taught herself to write and to dressmake by correspondence, she had saved enough money to buy a sowing machine and she was a very good cook indeed. All this inspite of ill health, at least partly due to the deprivation she had suffered as a child.

After her two children had finished their primary schooling in Leleque, she and her husband sent them to a secondary school in Esquel, paying their board, and then on to tertiary level. Their son now works as an accountant in the city of Trelew. The second child a girl, has finished secondary and has not yet decided between accountancy and teaching.

Aldina is my, and her own, big success story.

Chapter Seven

Leleque Estancia

The worst part of leaving Maiten was seeing old Cruz , the gardener, with tears running down his wrinkled cheeks and leaving Negro, Moira's cat. We told her we were coming back for him. We did not tell her that this depended on Negro himself. We did not want him attempting to cross fifty kilometres of lonely country on his own.

I never saw or heard of Cruz again. It was sad the way a move cut across this sort of close, working relationship. Negro's story ended happily. When we went back a week later he wouldn't let Moira out of his sight and jumped into the car with us without hesitation when we left. The new cook in Maiten had her own fat tom with a speck of black on his white nose; Negro had been very much second cat. In Leleque he found himself a new sleeping place under the wood burning stove in the kitchen. He died of old age and is buried with other of our special animals beneath a pine tree by the drive.

The Leleque property was 72 square leagues in area. It ran 4000 head of Hereford cattle, 1000 horses counting stallions, mares and working horses, and 60.000 Australian Merino sheep. It had the premier Australian Merino stud in South America. The Argentine Southern Land Company on the advice of their General Manager, Bill Mackinnon, were the first to import Australian Merino sheep into South America, sometime in the 1920's. Southern Patagonia is Corriedale country; the winters are too severe for Australian Merino lambs.

The blood of rams bred in Leleque stud ran in every important Australian Merino sheep stud in Argentina. Sheep farmers from all over South America came to buy rams and hoggets. The wool the Company produced on its properties was bought by firms in North America, Asia and Europe

Leleque homestead, a village of some twenty families, was crisscrossed by single, double and triple rows of Lombardy poplars planted to protect it from the wind that blew with particular force through a gap in the Sta Rosa range that looked down on the homestead from the west. Once it blew several carriages of the trencito where it passed infront of the gap, off the rails.

Along the Sta Rosa a band of trees ran beneath the snow line; eastwards the valley in which the homestead lay rose gently to treeless hills. A stream, the Leleque, ran past the homestead and on to join the river Chubut that curved round the foot of chunky hills that closed the valley to the north. Some way beyond the river ran the fence that divided Leleque estancia from the Indian reservation of Cushamen that supplied most of the labour.

The manager's house in Leleque, unlike the one in Maiten, was separated by fields from the rest of the homestead. The staff house, assistant manager's and book-keeper's houses, the store, garages and offices, machine sheds and police station, the huge piles of uncut wood for heating in winter and cooking all the year round, lay in uncrowded proximity to the stream.

A road, the Ruta Cuarenta, crossed the stream on a bridge and ran on through the homestead making a right angled turn past the manager's house with its orchards, hen run and vegetable garden. The bunk house faced the police station across the road near the bridge; behind it a row of well spaced foremen's cottages ran off at an angle.

The shearing and bull sheds were settled in their own clumps of trees several kilometres to the north; in the opposite direction were the sheep stud and the post office. With the wattle willows that bordered the stream they made a long, broken row of trees in that wide and windy pre-Cordillera valley.

Infront of the manager's house the back and front drives met round an oval lawn in which stood two big hawthorn trees. The private drive that ran between rows of hawthorn trees to a white gate on the road, was hardly ever used. Most people preferred to dodge the gate and come in through a yard past garages and stables, and up the poplar lined back drive. In old estancia houses in that part of Patagonia the entrance is often through the working parts of the farm. By the time a private entrance was made, if it was made, everyone was accustomed to the other.

Our house in Leleque was made of brick. It had a roof of tejuela, small tiles made of wood, and sash windows. The woodwork was painted green. The posts of the verandah that ran along the front of the house were wreathed in honeysuckle stems; in summer the flowers scented the air round the front door.

The house was built round three sides of a patio. The room we most used, leaving the drawing and dining rooms for formal occasions, was called the 'galeria'. It ran across the head of the patio. Originally a verandah, it had been glassed in and was full of light.. The windows looked over a lawn and rose bushes to a row of poplars. On summer evenings the roses seemed to expand and float in the gathering darkness; in winter the evening star rose over the blue line of the Sta Rosa and shone through the leafless poplars.

To one side of the house and at the back lawns and flowerbeds were enclosed and divided by a fence made of wooden slats with an ornamental pattern carved along the top. The horizontal cross bars to which the slats were nailed were covered with cushions of moss and litchens among which wrens hopped and picked and sang in the warmer months.

On the other side of the house was a walled yard that reminded me of the yard behind Uncle Frank's house in Devon, without the cobbles. Built round it were a luggage room, a dairy, a wash house, the shed that housed the electric light engine and, finally, by the door that led into the back drive, a wood pile. One of the minor frictions of daily life was between the woodmen who had their neat piles of cut wood unbalanced and careless, naughty or diminutive girls who, instead of stretching to take a piece from the top , grabbed the first that came to hand.

In the big, bright kitchen with its wood burning stove there was enough working surface for four people to chop or knead or beat without getting in each others' way. Near it there were rooms for china, glass and linen, for keeping tins of eggs preserved in times of abundance for seasons of scarcity, for grinding and mincing machines. There was a cool room.

The meat safe was on the far side of the back drive in a field crossed by clothes lines into which our children's horses sometimes blundered. It was in the shelter of a row of poplars. Cerda, the milkman, was 'alunado', that is to say he was affected by the phases of the moon. Normally a steady worker, if taciturn and unsociable, when the moon was full he might pull out the sticks neatly arranged over rows of young peas, take the first ripe tomatoe from the greenhouse or slice the undercut from a joint that I was keeping for guests expected the next day. No one saw him at his tricks, —milkmen work when most of us are asleep – but we all knew that it was he. I kept a very careful watch on the meat safe if I had a joint there and the moon was full.

On one such occasion, rather late, I went out in my dressing gown to have a look at the meat safe before going to bed. I crossed the drive and shone a torch on the joint. As I stood there in the shadow of the poplars that lay black across the moonlit grass a twig cracked sharply in the silence. When I emerged from the shadow into the drive I startled the two girls, cook and maid, who were coming home after visiting on the homestead. That made three of us, perhaps four. The joint was not touched that night.

When my predecessor in Leleque, whose husband was going to Pilcaneu estancia as General Manager in Don Mauricio's place, showed me round the house she took me out of the kitchen door to see the staff bathroom and other dependencies. When we came to a bare, bright room with a print of The Angelus hanging on a wall she said firmly, she was a firm sort of woman,

"This is Mary's room. I dont know who Mary was or why she had this room but that is what I was told when I took over this house and so now I am telling you."

Mary's room it remained. There was no need to pass on the information to my successor, she had lived long enough in Leleque to know the house almost as well as I did, but tradition is tradition and in the Company tradition mattered.

It took some months to get settled in our new home. Charlie had worked in Leleque before but had to get things going his way. With three small children, gardeners and domestic staff to adjust and adjust to, I had little time for comparisons and regrets. Dear Leleque! We spent twenty happy years there.

In Charlie the Australian ethic that any man, as a man, is as good as any other, that his worth lies in what he is rather than his education or background, was strongly developed. He treated the men under him as equals ("Call me Charlie", he'd say to the consternation of some nervous new recruit), no better and no worse except as they did

43

their jobs badly or well.

Along with this feeling that any man is as good as another went a profound belief in authority on the job. Bosses were to be obeyed. Hierachy, like tradition, was important in the Company. The Managing Director came at the top then the rest of the Board and on down through General Manager, Manager, office men, camp assistants, foremen, shepherds..... I dont mention the women who played such an important part in the success or failure of their husband's lives. Patagonia was a man's world.

Brought up among farmer's who owned their own land, the freest, most individual people in the world if not the richest, with nothing to push them around but the weather, and with English attitudes to class and education I had a lot to learn and understand.

The emphasis on hierachy and tradition suited the paisanos who made up the greater part of the work force. As I have said the paisano was a mixture of indigenous blood –mostly Araucano and Tehuelche in that part of Argentina—and European, mostly Spanish. The indigenous peoples had lived in tribes where the strongest and cleverest was head and gave the orders, though decisions affecting the whole group were made in open parliament. Many years later, long after Charlie had retired, a man who lived near Leleque said to me,

"I never heard a paisano speak ill of Don Guillermo." In the Company Charlie was always Don Guillermo.

Stealing infuriated him, nor did he put up with dirtiness or laziness, but if a man was in real trouble he could rely on sympathetic treatment. Then again, if some farm-hand asked him for a small loan he was pretty sure to get it. Charlie, careful with Company money, was quite easily separated from his own.

Any sort of chicanery sickened him. On the only occasion I know of when he paid a few pesos to a policeman to avoid a long wait when we were held up late at night and the children were tired, it made him physically sick. The only man stupid enough to offer him a bribe had to get off the estancia in a hurry. On these occasions I remembered the generations of Mackinnon incumbents of a manse on the Isle of Skye from whom he was descended.

My father's attitude to this sort of thing was quite different. A man of principle himself he accepted that others were not and did not allow it to worry him. Once, in England, he took the train from Devon up to London determined to see a test match at Lords Cricket Ground that started next day. Everyone told him that it was a waste of time, he had no chance of getting in, the tickets had been sold out for weeks ahead. My father said nothing but off he went.

He found a taxi driver who, for a consideration, agreed to take him into Lords through a back entrance. He stood for as long as his feet would support him, then he got a row of indignant schoool boys to push up and give him room at the end of a bench. He really enjoyed the cricket.

But my father must have a chapter to himself.

Chapter Eight
Don José

One afternoon in the late twenties of this century a car with the small bonnet, canvas hood and general horseless carriage look of the time, was bouncing along a straight, dirt road across the plains of central Argentina.

An observant or intuitive person might have guessed from the expression in his blue eyes that the driver was not a patient man. His high, broad forehead that extended into a bald head fringed with soft, brown hair gave some indication of a keen brain and his powerful chest and shoulders were those of an athlete, but nothing in his appearance revealed the outrageous sense of humour, the Puck within that sober exterior. With his battered grey hat, open necked shirt and roomy grey flannels held at the waist by a broad belt he looked what he was, a respectable, middle aged estanciero.

His expression at the moment was thoughtful. Though his large hands and powerful wrists guided the car efficiently his mind was not on the job. It had no need to be, he knew every clump of trees, every mud hole and windmill on that stretch of plain, a good deal of which had belonged at one time or another to members of his family.

A rugby team from the British Isles was touring Argentina. Members of the British Community had been asked to send invitations which were distributed among the players according to whether they wished to see one part of the country or another, or preferred more sophisticated entertainment. The invitation sent by Don José had been accepted for four young men and he was now on his way to meet them.

As he drove away from the low, verandahed house that had grown from the bare block of rooms made by his father, he noticed that it was not looking its best. The lawn was parched and brown for lack of rain, the trees were bare of leaves and so were the creepers that in summer varied and softened the cream coloured walls. The character of the house was, in any case, homely comfort rather than elegance.

He drove down the tree lined drive and out onto the road, turning south after a few kilometres onto a straight road that led directly to the town at which his guests were due to arrive. The road led through low, swampy land between reeds and clumps of pampas grass inhabited by birds and cuis, little brown, tailless creatures that ran across the road infront of the car. The fences on either side, one or two sagging wires attatched to twisted posts, showed the opinion the owners held of that undrained land by the little they were prepared to spend enclosing it. Tracks smoothed by car tires on the rough surface of hard baked clay wandered from side to side of the road avoiding the worst patches. In the very lowest part a bridge humped over the clods of a dried out pond.

A little further on a wretched adobe shack of a kind no longer seen in that part of the province of Sta Fé, stood beside a stretch of muddy water, a year round breeding place for mosquitos, across from an equally delapidated shed. Further on still the land started to rise. It was as flat as ever but the soil improved as did the fences and the type and condition of the stock. Clumps of trees sheltered well made farmhouses.

By the time was driving through the dirt streets of a country town the thoughtful look with which Don José started his journey was gone.

There was a smile on his lips and a look in his eyes that would have warned his wife had she been with him instead of making the final arrangements for the comfort of her guests, that anything might happen. Puck was in possession.

The four young rugger players were bored and dusty after their journey; a day of travelling across endless plains broken by clumps of trees, for variety a sulky jogging along the road by the railway or a car, perhaps, trailing a plume of dust that drifted off across fields of new green; stops in identical stations where, on platforms edged by heavily pruned trees, the citizens of little towns paraded solemnly.

The descended thankfully and were warmly greeted by their host, a fair skinned, country English looking sort of man immediately recognisable among the mediterranean faces on the platform. In no time they and their luggage were swept through the station and into a car that stood in the light shade of leafless trees outside.

He chatted knowledgeably about the country and its inhabitants as they drove along a dusty earth road. In the intervals of polite conversation they had pleasant thoughts of cool drinks and the bath that would presently wash away the dust of their journey which was being overlaid by more from the clouds that swirled round the interior of the car.

They were taken by surprise when the car turned in through a gateless opening in the run down wire fence by the road and came to stop infront of a miserable adobe shack. Surprise gave way to shock when their host announced cheerfully,

"Here we are."

A stout, sweaty woman wearing a garment that hung limply where it did not bulge, appeared in the doorway. She was surprised to see Don José and more surprised when four frozen faced young men got out of the car and shook her hand. A number of dirty children gathered round to watch this odd ceremony. They had no means of knowing that Don José, who avoided lies, was saying,

"Meet the wife."

There was an uncomfortable pause while he smiled benignly on the little group, then, taking leave of his unwitting wife in Spanish he turned to the Englishmen.

"Get back in and we'll take the luggage round to your room," he said, indicating the shed on the other side of the pond. They did as they were told, were driven round the pond and out onto the road again.

Telling the story in after years my father, alias Don José, would recall between chuckles and snorts of laughter that for a full five minutes after leaving the shack by the pond there was silence in the car. Then someone started to laugh. Chirú must have looked a palace after that shack which was, of course, what my father intended.

Joe Traill was three years old when Robert and Edmund, his uncle and father lost almost all they owned in the Baring crisis of the eighteen nineties and Edmund, stranded moneyless in England with no hope of further remittances borrowed money to pay his own and his family's passages back to Argentina to start all over again.

The house they came to was a block of four rooms, two on either side of a passage. It was made of uncooked bricks plastered with mud and whitewashed. The roof of corrugated iron sloped back from a low parapet. There may have been a few trees in the bare earth round that speck on the sea of plain.

One can imagine what the young wife –she was considerably younger than her husband—must have felt when she saw her new home. One can be equally certain that she concealed her feelings. Deeply religious, a devoted mother and wife, she was the centre round which her family revolved. I do not think that she was a typical, down

49

to earth pioneer wife. She drew, carved and played the organ.

The children ran ragged. Their hair was cut into some sort of shape with the help of a pudding bowl. They had rice pudding every day; galleta and other stores were brought by bullock cart from Cañada de Gomez with the mail once a fortnight, a three day trek either way.

Both Edmund and his wife were the children of clergymen. They worried about their children's upbringing, the pioneer atmosphere, the lack of schooling. Once, when Edmund's family was growing and his wife, who was expecting a child, was intensely pre-occupied about the education of those she already had a young woman appeared out of the blue to offer herself as governess. My father never forgot his father's anger when this young man proved to be a lively young man playing a joke.

The parental concern about their children's education, a woman so cleverly impersonated as to deceive all the family, recalls a similar episode in one of the early chapters of Far Away and Long Ago. Perhaps my father's childhood on the plains of Sta Fé was not so different from W.H. Hudson's south of Buenos Aires fifty years earlier.

While Joe was growing up there was little money to spare; he had no formal education. He was a clever man. Perhaps it was this lack of training for an active brain that made him quirky and unconventional.

He was seventeen when he was left in charge of Chirú while his parents took Auntie Agnes and the three younger sons to England to be educated at Charterhouse and university. That year the remittance man (that is to say a person whose family remitted him money from abroad, often because he was an embarrassment to his family), who lived to the north of Chirú in a disused railway carriage was killed. This kind old man was fond of animals and ploughed at night so that his mules should not suffer from the heat. One night he fell infront of the plough and the mules took fright pulling it over him.

The body was stiff by the time it was found and kept slipping off the sulky in which my father took it to the nearest cemetry, four leagues away.

In the last years of the nineteenth century and the beginning of the twentieth the world situation favoured the Argentine farmer; money came easily. My father had time on his hands and he devoted it to sport. He and his cousins, Robert's sons, spent as much time on horseback as off. Polo came to them as naturally as it did to the Persians who originated the game. They often drove their horses forty or fifty kilometres for a week end's polo. When, in the last decade of the nineteenth century, two of Robert's sons were playing in the Championship of the River Plate, as the Argentine Open Championship was then called, they drove their horses 500 kilometres to the station Media Luna, later re-named Halsey, in the Province of Buenos Aires where they were loaded onto a train together with those of the other members of the team.

A team of four Traills, my father and three cousins, won the Argentine Open Championship, the most important title in world polo today, three times and reached the finals in five consecutive years, 1904 to 1908 inclusive. Joe was in the winning team on several other occasions.

In their late fifties Robert and Edmund still had plenty of energy and zest. When a team of four Traills won the Championship of the River Plate for the first time the great news was telegraphed to Chirú and Las Limpias, Robert's home, immediately after the deciding game. The brothers each had a messenger waiting at their nearest stations and their fastest trotters –they did not ride very well- tied in. The telegrams arrived at the two houses more or less simultaneously and each brother set out at full speed to carry the news to the other. When they met they were travelling too fast to pull up and drove in circles over the plain shouting and cheering like schoolboys.

The Traills played in England, though not as a team, and represented both Argentina and Ireland in different tournments. Their hard riding and long hitting brought Argentine polo to the notice of the world. The Argentine government showed its appreciation when it offered to bring back the players and their ponies in a naval vessel, the Rivadavia, in 1912 after a particularly successful season in the British Isles.

My father, a country boy, was catapulted into the highest levels of English social life while still in his teens.. I dont think it worried him much. Playing polo at a club in England his horse tripped and fell and he came off running in classic gaucho style. The people watching applauded so he did a sommersault or two to end off with.

He had some embarrassing moments. While in Dublin the team was invited to a meal at the Vice regal Lodge after representing Ireland in a tournament which they won. Strawberries were served towards the end of the meal. My father <u>loved</u> strawberries. He quickly mashed them. In need of a spoon he looked up and saw that everyone else at the long table lined by footmen was picking up the berries one by one and dipping them into little dishes of cream and sugar that stood by each plate. It was one of the most uncomfortable moments of his life he told me.

In Dublin he met my mother, Audrey Lawson, the daughter of the Manager of Guiness's Brewery. Though her father was of Scottish extraction and her mother was English she had a very Irish gaiety and charm. She loved people, parties, presents, the happy things; ladies and gentlemen, shop assistants and waiters all responded to her friendly charm.

She shared my father's interest in sport. On her desk at Chirú, beside the photograph of her receiving her degree at Trinity College,

Dublin, stood one of her school hockey team in high necked blouses and full black skirts, their hair upswept in the fashion of that time. Playing in a tennis tournament in southern England my father and mother came up against Fred Perry, the most successful tennis player of his time, and his partner, the then ladies champion of England. My parents took a set off them before they adjusted to my father's power (one shot knocked the raquet out of Perry's hand) and my mother's quickness.

"Then, of course," my mother would say, "They set about us."

She was a courageous woman which was just as well, married as she was to a man who would back his own strength and quickness against the odds and might do something fairly outrageous if the humour took him. If she heard a suspicious sound from the hen run at night she would get out of bed, put on a dressing-gown, pick up a torch and investigate.

I remember a time when the bus we were in was crawling along the top of a steep embankment, the dirt road slippery after rain. The bus skidded and teetered on the edge. The driver wrestled with the steering wheel and suddenly we found ourselves, upright still, facing the way we had come. The first sound to break the shocked silence in the bus was my mother's delighted laughter.

Joe was fairly alarming as a father; one could not be sure what he might do. He was a quick eater and while he waited for the rest of the family to finish would roll the bread left on his side plate into little balls which he put in his coat pocket to harden. At home he would amuse himself and us by flicking them up against the ceiling and saying, 'This one is for your cup so and so.' I cannot remember any landing on target.

In a restaurant in Buenos Aires, just to make things exciting for us, he might say, 'See that woman with a red feather in her hat?' And a pellet would go pinging across the tables not actually aimed at the red feather, I now think. On a liner crossing the Atlantic he had people at the table he had chosen as a target gazing at the air vent above it. The Chief Engineer, whose table it was, was not amused when my father, who expected others to share his sense of humour, told him the origen of the mysterious missiles.

Government officials affected my father in the way they affect most farmers, that is to say negatively. During Peron's years as president Joe was having a meal in the local town, San Jorge, when a self-important individual in a car with a government number plate walked in and ordered a drink at the bar. My father sitting at one of the tables, aimed a bread pellet at the ceiling above him and made the shot of his life. The pellet dropped down into the man's glass.

The official, furious at being made to look ridiculous, turned on the young man at the table next my father's —perhaps Joe looked too respectable or too formidable. The young man was so obviously innocent and bewildered that the rest of the people in the restaurant took up arms on his behalf and the official retired angry and unfed. My father's skin had been saved again. I think he was more careful after that.

It is tempting to remember Joe for his mischievous tricks and not for the intelligence and effort he put into keeping the family farm going through good times and bad. My brother and sister were at school in England at the time of the Depression. My father and mother were only able to keep them there by making severe economies. They also took on lads from England whose parents paid to have them taught farming —in some cases to get them off their hands. The boys lived and ate with us. One had some kind of a nervous crisis and had to be taken off in a hurry after a night spent wandering round the house with a gun under his arm.

In Peron's time my father's interest in and knowledge of the law kept Chirú intact when many farms changed hands or were broken up. At that time the name of the station on the line that ran past Chirú was changed from Traill to Evita. It became Traill again after 1955.

My father could be very understanding. When I was eleven I was sent to a boarding school in the suburbs of Buenos Aires. After I had been there for a month or two I was told that my father was coming to see me. I was sure he would appear in bombachas and that the girls would laugh at him. What a relief it was to see him in a dark suit and a tie! When I was old enough to tell him this he took it to heart and never behaved in anything but the most sedate and respectable way when visiting me at school.

He enjoyed his daughter's weddings and would appear at the head of the aisle with the bride on his arm looking the proudest of fathers in the dark suit he called his wedding suit. He could not be persuaded into tails.

With all his gifts and abilities my father, like most people who are secure in themselves, was genuinely modest. He might at times find others a bit slow but never thought himself clever. Neither he nor my mother allowed the tragedy that shadowed the last years of their lives, the death of their only son in the Second World War, to crush them.

Chapter Nine

A Country School

Our children did their first years of schooling in a little building that kept company with the station five kilometres from Leleque homestead. Every day they waited for the pick up at the end of the hawthorn drive –all except Joan who preferred to get ready earlier and get on in the yard with the rest of the school children. They went off looking clean and fresh in their white coats and returned considerably less so. White does not stand up well to dusty playgrounds.

Two teachers taught the primary grades to thirty or forty children aged between six and fifteen. Nowadays, I'm told, there are few country day schools in lonely parts of the province of Chubut. Where possible children are collected in bigger schools where they board at government expense. This is a good idea even apart from the question of diet; distances are so great. Little children who had to go several kilometres back and forth each day on horseback or on foot lost a lot of days through illness, bad weather or lack of transport. A poor family did not have horses to spare.

In country schools in Patagonia the school year ran through the warmer months; from September to the end of May, with a fortnight's break over the 'fiestas' as the Christmas, New Year holiday season was called. The winter months of June, July and August were a quiet time in every way.

The level of intelligence and attendance among the pupils at Leleque school was high as country schools went because they were, for the most part, children of people who held a steady job in the Company so were well fed and the pick up took them to school each day. A few were very poor, the children of squatters on a piece of fiscal land near the school.

"She's so poor, Mummy, that no one will sit with her."

I should have been warned. Poverty is no stigma in that part of the world. Before long Moira's head started to itch. We tried various unpleasant home remedies before getting rid of the lice with a powder normally used on hens.

In Leleque we kept up our tradition of Christmas parties though, as there were so many children, I cut it down to girls only, otherwise filling Father Christmas' sack came too expensive. Our new Father Christmas –David was managing estancia San José in central Patagonia—was again an unexpected volunteer. Pedro Buttazzi, like the Leleque store he looked after, was a Company tradition.

Anyone who has lived in Argentina will have a picture in his or her mind of the 'boliche de campo', the country pub cum store; the iron bars to protect the storeman, the small windows, the long counter. Leleque store only had bars on the door and windows as alcoholic drinks were not sold there, but it carried people back to the Wild West period of Argentine history. A wooden counter ran the length of a long, narrow, rather dark room, on it, at the end nearest the door an ornate, old fashioned cash register. The shelves on the wall behind were filled with bombachas, alpagatas, boots, shirts, berets, hats, neckerchiefs..... On the floor behind the counter were bins holding basic foodstuffs: yerba, rice, sugar, flour.

Apart from the usual tinned tomatoes, oil, vinegar, spices and so on there were knives, ponchos, saddle clothes, and 'bastos' the base for the recado, the pile of saddle clothes topped by a sheepskin on which the men rode, and other articles of interest to country people. Over the door outside was a painted sign about a metre square with the name of the Company painted in black on a white ground round the edge. In the centre was the circle S, the Company brand.

To birthday parties our children now brought all their class from school, each child with some tiny gift. We progressed from dancing and singing in a circle on the lawn to races and dressing up. On these occasions I asked Mariucha to give me a hand. Mariucha taught the younger children at the school. She boarded with Don Ricardo and his wife, Doña Mercedes, in the last of the row of foremen's cottages. Dick, as Don Ricardo was sometimes called, was one of the oldest members of the Leleque work force, a slight, erect man with a dignified manner. He was in charge of the pedigree ewe flocks. In spring Doña Mercedes' kitchen was full of lambs.

Mariucha was an exceptionally pretty girl. Neither pretty girls nor good causes were common in Leleque. When she decided to collect money for a children's party at the school to end the year all wallets opened wide. She collected so much money that she came to ask me if I thought she should accept it. On the first birthday party she came to at home we had team races, she and I starting off for our teams. Out of consideration for my age —about forty—she started off slowly. I had always enjoyed games and running and left her far behind. The next time she was ready for me and we tied.

The time I tried an Easter party it was not a success. The children came to tea; then I set them looking for Easter eggs which I had hidden in the orchard. I had hidden them too well. In the end we were all searching and the children got quite desperate. Eventually we found all but the one hidden farthest from the house. It was discovered, in small country communities everything comes out in the end, that a

group of small boys had been seen lurking near the orchard that afternoon. It was unfair, they felt, that their sisters should have all the parties and all the presents.

The Leleque school was about two leagues from the homestead, a
small, exposed building made smaller still by the scale of the surroundings; the wide valley on whose eastern slopes it stood and the Cordillera opposite. Buckets of water poured by the children in recreation
periods on the trees planted ten years earlier to shelter it, had suc-
ceeded only in keeping them alive.

The school year when our children began their schooling ended
officially on the 31st of May, actually on the 25th. El Veintecinco was
an important date on the estancia calendar As well as being the most
deeply rooted in popular feeling of Argentina's national holidays it was
the virtual end of the school year.

The teachers, together with a group of parents arranged the
programme. The proceedings were meant to start at ten in the morning with a show put on by the pupils who were then treated to a feed
of cakes washed down with hot chocolate. There followed an asado
that might include dancing to a guitar or accordion. The celebrations
ended with horse racing and games. The twenty fifth of May is less
than a month off the shortest day of the year, it was not easy to fit all
this into just one of them.

The sun was hardly over the north eastern horizon when we made
our way from the homestead, cakes and salads balanced on our knees,
over roads slippery with mud or frozen stiff, towards the schoolhouse.
Everyone was headed in the same direction, every vehicle on or around
the homestead and horsemen in their smartest gear, wide brimmed
hats, crisp bombachas and shining boots, bridles and belts studded
with silver. All the women took something, cakes for the children or
salads to accompany the asado.

It was not easy to produce a good cake at that time of the year. By May even the most devoted hen had gone of the lay and as most of the milk had been kept back for several days for the children's chocolate (I suspected Cerda of using it as an excuse to take a rest from separating) there was little butter. It took some foresight and ingenuity to produce a cake that would pass muster when handed in under the critical scrutiny of the women gathered outside the door of the school kitchen. Salads were made of beetroot, carrots, onions or tinned vegetables.

It was usually well past eleven by the time the flag had risen to the mast-head on the frail voices of two rows of well combed children singing the Cancion a la Bandera. Not all had white coats. This did not seem to worry them but sad the child that was not wearing something new on its feet that day. Once the flag was flying we crowded into the two classrooms that had been opened into one and decorated with blue and white streamers. Chairs and benches accomodated some of the audience.

We put our hearts into the National Anthem, listened to a patriotic discourse by one of the teachers and waited, looking at the curtain that had been hung across the room. It usually parted jerkily on one or more of the youngest children who, like young children everywhere, were warmly applauded. But even those of a more self-conscious age, even the few who could hardly get through a line without help from the prompter, got a hearty clap. For some it was the only entertainment of the kind they ever attended and it was a responsive audience, if a noisy one. It was seldom that one of the little brothers or sisters present was not talking or crying.

The show lasted for two and a half to three hours and consisted of recitations, sketches, dancing and, sometimes, singing. Most of the people there had names of Spanish or indigenous origin, their features

60

were European or American in about equal proportions. Almost all the children were dark, including a family by the name of Thorpe, descended probably from a worker on the railway when it was British owned. The red heads of Pedro Buttazzi's children shone out like torches. Our children were lighter haired than most but their gestures were as wooden, their voices as monotonous as the rest. The words did not matter. What mattered was not to forget them. The only school child I heard recite with a feeling for the words was an older girl with an attractive voice and a composed presence who came, I was told, from the indigenous community of Cushamen.

Outside the window the Santa Rosa glittered with frozen snow. Inside it grew more and more stuffy. Most of the men stood near the door making excursions into the biting cold outside where loaded asadores leaned inwards in a circle over embers raked from a huge fire. The younger ones enjoyed heckling a companion, some young man of fifteen who was finishing his primary education. Most of them had given up years before, to the relief of their parents. Their victim would fix his eyes on the wall above our heads and battle through his piece, a hunted look crossing his face when he lost the thread, one of relief when he picked it up again.

Every now and then one of the older men would shout, "Viva la Patria."

What the audience enjoyed most were the sketches, where the speaking and movements were much more natural than in the recitations. The Spanish lady and her 'criada', the street vendor in colonial Buenos Aires, held the attention but what really brought the house down were the humorous sketches: the browbeaten conscript slyly getting his own back on the sergeant, the two deaf men in conversation. The naughty boy of the homestead dressed as an estanciero or a policeman had everyone laughing before he opened his mouth.

What the children enjoyed most were the dressing up and the dancing; boys zapateando manfully but, as the stage was not raised, invisibly to all but those on the front benches, girls with unsmiling faces and coquettish handkerchiefs dancing the cueca or the gato. I never felt closer to that first, grey, drizzling Veinticinco de Mayo in 1810.

The least effective teachers were usually older, people whose interest in their work had not survived years in lonely little schools teaching children who had never seen a book, whose parents considered the years spent in educating their children an irritating waste of time forced on them by the government. Many years later when Moira was sixteen or seventeen she stood in for one of the teachers for a week or two. She described her efforts to get a conversation going in class. She tried various subjects; toys and fairy stories meant nothing to the children, food and parents something quite different, it was only when she spoke of the plants and bushes that grew on the hillsides they lived among that everyone had something to say.

At the other end of Leleque estancia from the homestead, just outside the boundary, rose the cream coloured walls of a school where forty children boarded at government expense during the school year. They were the children of peasant farmers who eked out a living in a particularly desolate area. The attractive young couple who were in charge of the school that, seven years after it was built had only just been connected with the outside world by a proper road, came to a farewell asado given for the foreman in charge of the section of the estancia across the river Chubut from the school.

"Teaching these children," she told me, "Is like making marks on a clean slate. The children who come to us have never slept in a bed, eaten with a fork, washed regularly or used lavatory paper. They leave and go back to that again. Sometimes I wonder if our work is worth while."

"It must be," I cried, and turned to Enrique, the foreman, a man of wisdom and experience. "What do you think?"

He looked thoughtfully across the valley to the school and said,

"Twenty years ago there was no school."

Apart from Mariucha, an energetic and hard working teacher, I remember two others. One was a young man with an arm crippled by infantile paralysis who was the first to rouse in Moira the interest in things of the mind which she has never lost. The other became, thirty years later, Secretary for Culture in the Municipality of Esquel. When he played on the guitar and sang for them the children clustered round him, their normally stolid little faces alight. I remember his remarking of his pupils with satisfaction,

"They have become quite naughty. They have learned to play."

When our daughters were eight or nine years old and had finished the third grade of primary school it seemed necessary to give them a higher level of education. While Don Mauricio was General Manager he had suggested to the Board that managers should be helped with the education of their children as on their salaries they could not afford boarding school fees. As a bachelor his advice was obviously disinterested. Thanks to him the Company paid what began as three quarters of boarding school fees and ended as something more than half.

We sent our children to a boarding school in Bariloche where the curriculum included English as well as Spanish. The only real sorrow I suffered in our years in Leleque was sending them away.

Chapter Ten

Woodville School

San Carlos de Bariloche, then a town of some 25.000 inhabitants, was about two hundred kilometres north and slightly west of Leleque. It was different. It did not seem to belong in the Patagonia of thirty years ago. Esquel, El Maiten, El Bolson, Trelew, were towns or cities that had grown in response to the needs of the local population, or through an influx of people caused by the making of a road or a railway. Bariloche lived off and for tourists. Communications were good; the comforts that tourists expect and pay for arrived by road, rail and air.

Some country people disliked Bariloche for its sophistication. During his six or seven years as General Manager of The Southern Land Company Don Mauricio, living an hour's run away in Pilcaneu, only went to Bariloche when he needed a hair cut; he never so much as had a meal there. He was not typical. Most of us, male and female, enjoyed a bit of sophistication; a pick at the crumbs that fell from the tourist's table.

Even then Bariloche was known all over Argentina. It offered skiing as well as summer tourism. A community of Swiss and German origin knew how to attract and attend to tourists. Its lovely situation on lake Nahuel Huapi with the long line of the Cordillera behind, the facilities and easy going life style attracted artists and writers and other interesting and unusual people. The products of cottage industries: different sorts of jam made from berries that grew locally, pottery, figures made from wood or stones, candles with leaves and flowers embedded in the wax, Bariloche chocolate and Bariloche knits filled the shop windows in Mitre, the long, main street. There was a pleasant oddness about the people in the streets. Today we are accustomed to tourists, in the 1960's they were unusual and fun.

A few years before our children reached the age where they needed more than Leleque school could provide, a couple of experienced school teachers from Buenos Aires started a boarding school in Bariloche for children whose parents wanted them to have a grounding in English as well as Spanish.

The school was called Woodville and stood on the wooded slopes above Lake Nahuel Huapi. The owners, Mr and Mrs Cohen, were excellent teachers and deeply religious. They had an old fashioned attitude to schooling; plain food, discipline, keeping children occupied, no fuss. Television was frowned on; the children went for long walks on holidays. There was little or no organised sport. When our children finished primary and went on to school in Buenos Aires they were on a par or ahead of their companions scholastically and a gifted teacher had given them an interest in music, but the only sport in which they could compete with the other girls was skiing. Not much use in Buenos Aires.

When our children were told, as they often were, how lucky they were to be at school in such a beautiful place, they took it as yet another example of the stupidity of grown ups. How could school be beautiful? There were two terms of four months each. Winter holidays were the month of July, summer holidays December, January and Febuary; there was a three or four day exeat in the middle of each term.

It was a four hour drive from Leleque to Bariloche along a winding mountain road that must have been one of the most beautiful in Argentina. There was another road outside the mountains through Ñorquinco and Pilcaniyeu, it was longer but took about the same time because it was less trafficked and less dangerous. In bad weather, and many of our drives to and from Bariloche neccssarily took place in winter, the inner or mountain road was the safest. It was less lonely and was kept open after a snowfall.

Leaving Leleque one crossed fifty kilometres of open country before dropping down into the straggling village of Epuyen at the head of a lake that wound westwards into the mountains. Out of Epuyen the road wound up a steep, piney hill before dropping again into the lovely valley known as El Hoyo, home to many families of Polish origin. Beyond, over another rise, was the valley of El Bolson. These two valleys were fertile and windless, perfect for small farming, a complete contrast to the largely infertile, wind swept hills of the pre-Cordillera. They produced raspberries, strawberries hops and orchards of fruit trees. Walnut trees shaded the streets of El Bolson which is only 300 mts above sea level.

El Bolson was a cosmopolitan sort of town, after the style of Bariloche on a smaller scale. A good percentage of the inhabitants were of central European origin. There was an influx of hippies in the sixties who formed a colony outside the town. It still exists. An unusual sort of community for this part of the world at that time. Looking down on the town from the east is a dramatic ridge of rock called the Piltriquitron which means in Araucano, I have been told, 'purple coloured mountain always covered in mist'. I never noticed any mist in the summer months.

After El Bolson the road started to turn and twist and dance. According to an article in a national newspaper of the time there were

392 blind corners on the road between El Bolson and Bariloche. We took turns with other families from the Esquel area who sent their children to Woodville, in bringing and taking them. It was a nervy business driving that road with a car load of children. If Charlie was busy Ofelio Lopez, who had been Don Mauricio's chauffeur, was entrusted with the job. The journey was made longer by stops for car sickness and for spending pennies.

The highest point of the drive was the Pampa del Toro, 1700 mts above sea level. The road up to it wound up the side of a deep canyon called El Cañadon de la Mosca, a precipice on one side, a cliff on the other. Little streams fell through fern and thicket to the depths beneath and a crag pushed up from the floor of the canyon. A short, level stretch across the Pampa del Toro, another climb and then it was downhill to a string of lakes named after Jesuit missionaries, Guillelmo, Mascardi, Gutierrez, who crossed over from the Pacific side of the Andes in the 17th and 18th centuries to convert the indigenous peoples and lost their lives doing so.

Along lake Guillermo the road ran between a cliff and the lake which was very deep just there. If two vehicles met one of them had to back. Lake Mascardi that received the water from the Tronador glacier was a wonderful turquoise green. Forests of coihue (nothrofagus dombeyi), bushes of yellow flowering michai and orange lilies, amancay, bordered the road. The Tronador mountain takes its name from the sound of glacial ice adjusting to its infinitesimal progress. It is a name more in keeping with the surroundings than El Bolson or El Cañadon de la Mosca.

We set out early when we went to Bariloche to get the children out from school to get some shopping done before midday, have lunch and return as soon as we could get Mrs Cohen, who did not like children to miss classes, to let them go. In winter we never got back to

Leleque until well after dark.

We had a few frights on our journeys back and forth. Once when Charlie and I were going to fetch the children from school after a period of heavy rains we took all day to get to Bariloche, digging our way through landslides. We travelled in convoy with other stranded travellers. Everyone dug and drove alternately. Everyone, that is, except the Leleque storeman, Pedro Buttazzi's successor, to whom we were giving a lift, who, through dislike of manual work, fright or some medical reason he did not share with us, retired to the back of the car and slept. One difficult piece of road was a steep slope that had to be taken at speed. If the driver was too quick or too slow with the gear change the car slid back to the bottom.

We made some new friends that day. One uncomplaining lady from El Maiten was seriously ill, her husband was taking her to Bariloche for medical attention. A lawyer from Esquel whom I had always thought of as an office man dug and drove with the best. These two turned back when the car infront of us developed engine trouble. The worst part of the journey was Charlie's insistance on being the last in the convoy. I would have felt safer somewhere near the middle but he could not bear to have a car on his tail.

One would rather not have met anyone on the Cañadon de la Mosca at any time of the year as the road was not always wide enough to allow two vehicles to pass, nor was the outside edge always to be trusted, but the danger was obvious and even our summer driving hazard, tourists, took it seriously. In winter the stretches that never got the sun iced over. Once, when the road was in this condition, we were sliding cautiously down the Cañadon homeward bound with a car-load of hilarious children when a jeep poked its nose round the corner ahead. Both drivers applied their brakes carefully and without effect –gently, inevitably, we collided. The children thought it more hilarious still.

I was not present at the most dangerous moment of the many drives our children made between Leleque and Bariloche. When I remember myself cheerfully preparing for their arrival it astonishes me that we can be unaware when the lives of those we love are in danger.

Another parent was bringing our daughters home. They left Woodville at three o'clock of a winter afternoon, some of the children lying under rugs in the back of the pick up. It was growing dark when they took the steep curves down to the Foyel, a rushing river crossed by a wooden bridge. The floor of the bridge was frozen and the pick up skidded, hitting the wooden guard rail at one side and knocking it into the river before the driver was able to bring it under control.

"Do you know, Mummy," Joan remarked as a matter of interest, "We were in the back and when we sat up to see what had happened we saw the railing floating away down the river." Had the pick up gone over the edge they must all have been drowned.

It was on one of these drives that I saw my first and, I think, only UFO. We were on our way back from Woodville with a car full of children. It was already dark and most of them were asleep when we climbed the hill out of Epuyen and turned east for the last, straight-forward run home. I noticed what I took to be a fire on a slope to the south. One loses one's sense of direction on a winding road in the dark. I could never place the spot exactly afterwards. I commented on it to Moira and another girl who was awake. As we looked I noticed that there was no flicker of flames and the light was rather pale. Then I saw what looked to be fine, dark lines that crossed it at intervals; the whole shape of the fire, or light, was vaguely elliptical. By now we were looking at it out of the rear window of the car. Ofelio had his eyes firmly on the road ahead, and, looking at our sleepy passengers, I had no desire to tell him to stop so that we could examine whatever it was more closely.

I have never believed that little men with antenna step out of space ships, but one never knows; I was glad when, as I suppose, a hillside interrupted our view of whatever it was we had seen. It had occurred to me that if we could see them our lonely lights must be visible the other way. On our next drive that way and on many others, I looked for the scar of a burn on the mountain sides south of Epuyen, but I never found one.

Now the road from El Bolson to Bariloche is being paved. On the side of the Cañadon de la Mosca opposite the old road great scars have been torn to make a new one. I suppose that speed is important; that the sacrifice of beauty is necessary for the safety of the more and more tourists who visit us. I wish the road had been made outside the mountains, over the bare hills between Ñorquinco and Pilcaniyeu. Paved roads on long, empty stretches are a joy, among the mountains they destroy as much as they improve. Tourists who come to enjoy beauty could travel quietly along the old road and leave the new to those who count the minutes.

The three month summer holidays made us a family again. Looking back it seems that the sun was always shining when we spread the rug on a strip of sheltered lawn between the verandah and the drive and settled down to read. Happy memories make their own sunshine but December, January and Febuary, though sometimes cool and windy, were not normally cloudy in Leleque.

The custom of lying outside after lunch while I read aloud was one of those family routines that come into being in answer to a need. Children are easily bored; estancia life can be boring. Our daughters were close enough in age to be companions. They spent a lot of time on horseback during the summer holidays; trooping sheep, riding to the shearing shed to have mate and torta frita in the breaks, playing bandits in the woods of osier willow along the stream.

On a hot summer day there is a somnolent pause in the rythm of estancia life after the midday meal. Not only humans respect the siesta hour; horses stand dozing, sheep press together to make their own shade and hang their heads down into it, hens tuck down in drifts, birds are quiet and milch cows fold themselves down to the ground in that ungainly way. Children who do not rise at daybreak are unaffected by the general doziness, but the order was that until the bell rang for work the horses must rest; so we lay in the sun and read.

I ordered books from England in advance, searching my memory for books and writers that would entertain and at the same time leave something worth remembering. Ivanhoe, Tom Sawyer and Huckleberry Finn, The Jungle Books, The Refugees, The White Company, Jane Eyre, most of the books I had loved as a child retained their magic and our daughters loved some I had not, Vanity Fair, Oliver Twist and Wuthering Heights. Some were the actual books I had read as a child; Moonfleet inscribed in my grandmother's spidery hand, Kim, my father's gift, the leather cover stamped with a golden swastika reversed.

The advantage of reading aloud to children is that they can enjoy books far beyond their capacity to understand on their own. The story teller's gift transcends age and race but the written word raises barriers that melt when they are read aloud. Moira was twelve, Joan eleven and Flora eight when, finding myself short of reading material I started, rather doubtfully, on the famous opening sentence of Pride and Prejudice. 'It is a truth universally acknowledged that a single man in possession of a good fortune must be in want of a wife.' The book written nearly two hundred years earlier, using words and forms of words and assuming conventions long since gone, enthralled girls whose narrow experience of life had been gathered on an estancia and in a boarding school in Patagonia.

The custom in families of listening together while one of them read aloud was common in the days when books and entertainment were less easily come by. As entertainment it cannot compete with social activities, sport or television. It demands a steady rythm of life and a certain homogeneity of outlook in the listeners. A negative factor in our case was the difference in age which had to be catered to until Flora caught up with her sisters, a positive that the audience was entirely femenine. Most boys prefer stronger meat.

Tinker, the Border Collie, Lucky, a mongrel we had picked up on the road to Bariloche, and Negro always appeared round the corner of the house when the rug was spread and had no disrupting effect. Mickey, the Labrador who sometimes came to stay, always sat himself in the middle of the rug and had to be removed. Minute, golden ducklings that tilted their heads to keep one eye watchfully skywards and liked to shelter under a projecting chin, kittens born under the floor of the verandah that were tempted out with pieces of meat, distracted attention from the reading and I refused to compete. My concentration was sometimes disturbed by the thought of carefully tended rows of carrots and lettuces crushed under the horses' hooves as they grazed their way towards the grass that grew green and lush on the banks of the canals that watered the vegetable garden.

When school friends came to stay we almost always gave up our reading sessions because there was then no midday gap to fill. New companions meant new interests and things to do. Occasionally we carried on. An Australian girl whose father was in Bariloche as part of a United Nations project for Patagonia, was disappointingly uninterested in Kim, which we had already started when she arrived, until she happened to look at an illustration and realised that the Lama was not a llama.

Chapter Eleven

Musters

Walking along the main street in Bariloche one day when our daughters were at Woodville, I stopped to look into the window of a book shop and a title caught my eye, 'Vida entre los Patagones'. It was the translation into Spanish of a book written by George Chaworth Musters, published in London in 1871. The full title of the original was, 'At home with the Patagonians. A year's wandering over untrodden ground from the Straits of Magellan to the Rio Negro.'

This book was one of the best buys I ever made. I read the original years later. It was long out of print but a kindly Professor of Geography at the University of Alberta, who had spent a few days in Leleque while researching for a paper on immigration into Patagonia, found it and sent it to me. Funnily enough it was another Canadian, a traveller we had picked up on the road and brought home to tea, who sent me a copy of Lucas Bridges' book about Tierra del Fuego, The Uttermost Parts.

To return to Musters. The original was written in a stiff upper lipped Victorian style. Had I read it first I could not have appreciated the incredible discomforts and dangers of his journey nor been able to follow his route as I did with the translation, profusely annotated by an Argentine, Raul Rey Balmaceda, who followed Musters' steps as closely as possible.

George Chaworth Musters, an officer in the Royal Navy, was 27 years old when on a visit to the Malvinas Islands in 1869, he conceived the idea of travelling from south to north through the interior of Patagonia —at that time terra incognita. He crossed to the mainland, to Punta Arenas, and did the first 450 kilometres in April 1869, accompanying a Chilean expedition sent after prisoners escaped from the penal settlement in Punta Arenas.

This first stage of his journey ended on an island at the mouth of the river Sta Cruz. Isla Pavon, a trading station, had been set up by Luis Piedrabuena, one of the landmark figures in the history of European settlement in Patagonia. It was one of only three settlements on the Atlantic coastline of Patagonia. The others were the Welsh colony at the mouth of the River Chubut and Carmen de Patagones at the mouth of the Rio Negro.

Several tribes of Tehuelches with whom Piedrabuena traded spent the winter in the vicinity of Isla Pavon. When the worst of the winter was over some of them made the trip northwards over the spurs of the Andes to trade ostrich feathers and mantles of guanaco skin for woven articles, apples, piñones, the fruit of the araucaria, and chicha, an alcoholic drink made from fermented apples. The apple trees had been planted by Jesuit missionaries on proselytizing expeditions across the Andes from the Pacific coast in an area just north of Alicura, some 1500 kilometres from Isla Pavon. The Tehuelches were also planning to collect rations dispensed by the Argentine government.

Musters spent the months of deep winter on the island learning to live as the indians did, working his way into their confidence. This was not easy as, apart from being suspicious of Europeans in general, this group of Tehuelches was planning to have discussions with Araucano and Pampa indians farther north on how to deal with the

Europeans who were encroaching on their territory, spreading ever farther south and west.

Musters set off with his companions in early August when the wind off the Cordillera were cutting and the rivers they crossed were floating with chunks of ice. There were eighteen Tehuelche men with their wives and families. Musters dressed as his companions did in a chiripá and a mantle of guanaco skin held by a belt when riding. His notes on the scenery, on his companions and their customs, the rough maps he made calculating the position with a compass, had to be done as secretly as possible. The Tehuelches suspected anything they did not understand.

He was usually hungry and almost always cold. Years later an Indian woman said of him in pidgin Spanish,

"Musters mucho frio tenia. Muy bueno pobre Musters."

His digestion was not adapted to a diet of guanaco or ostrich meat eaten almost raw, roots when available and, as they got farther north, the odd fish and a few berries. Nor were his thin European skin and his circulation able to withstand the cold as did the Tehuelches', adapted over thousands of years to cold and discomfort.

He was often in danger of his life. His companions had little regard for life, human or animal, even when sober. As they got farther north they met people trading in aguadiente and chicha; drunken orgies took place with increasing frequency. That Musters lived to complete the 2750 kilometres from Punta Arenas to Alicura and then across the continent to Carmen de Patagones is more incredible even than his attempting it.

As I read on through the book, following Musters footsteps on a map, I began to recognise the sort of country in which he and his companions made their hunting circles and put up their tents or toldos. These, the rounded Mongolian type, were made of guanaco skins pulled over saplings in such a way as to make them curve over.

The group covered some 25 kilometres a day, the women and children on horseback keeping to age old tracks from camping place to camping place, the men scattering to hunt. There were stops to rest if someone became seriously ill, or to celebrate a birth or a girl reaching puberty. They could not stop for long because the herds of guanaco and ostrich on which they depended for food would move off. Any sign of other indians, smoke for instance, was cause for alarm; any group or individual was a potential enemy.

Musters and his companions came into what is now Leleque estancia near where Esquel airport is today. They travelled across Montoso section, crossed the river Lepa and all the streams that run eastwards from the Sta Rosa. The original group had been joined by others and some caciques had broken away. They were by now a mixture of Tehuelches and Araucanos.

They were in the Lepa area, some twenty kilometres from where Leleque homestead is today, when a messenger arived sent by Calfucurá, head of the Indians north of the Rio Negro in the area of Bahia Blanca. The message ran, 'My horse is ready; my foot is in the stirrup; my lance is in my hand and I go to make war against the Christians who tire us out with their falseness.'

The caciques called a parliament by the river Lepa. They deliberated and orated for some time infront of the assembled Indians, deciding eventually to have nothing to do with the affair. Calfucurá's message was a prelude to the raid on Bahia Blanca in 1871 that led to the Argentine government abandoning its policy of conciliating the caciques with gifts, and, finally, to General Roca's Conquest of the Desert Campaign of 1881 to 1883 that subdued and decimated the indigenous peoples of Patagonia

In Leleque, which Musters calls Lilly Haik, he and his companions took time off to wander in the woods, picking currants and edible fungus, relaxing and chatting among the yellow Patagonian violets and other wild flowers. They were moving very slowly because Crime, a cacique, had a badly infected leg and could hardly sit his horse. He died later.

When they crossed the river Chubut into Cushamen leaving Leleque behind Musters wrote, 'We bid adieu to the pleasant river and to the sylvan delights of this paradise as it seemed to us. As we ascended the northern declivity of the high ground bounding the valley I halted to take a farewell look and nowhere has a more beautiful scene presented itself to my gaze. The valley narrowed as it curved to the west and at its head, through a gigantic cleft, the perpendicular walls of which rose several hundred feet, the waters of the river issued from their mountain cradle.' Charlie told me that the scene described by Musters is in a part of Leleque known as Quince Sierras, where the river Chubut curves east at the foot of the chunky hills that close Leleque valley to the north.

The long straggling line of several hundred Indians with baggage horses carrying women, children, tents and belongings —one woman had a hen with her- travelled on across Cushamen, leaving the valley where the homestead and town of El Maiten keep company today, to the west. They carried on across the bare, open country between Ñorquinco and Pilcaniyeu that I got to know so well a hundred years later. Musters describes the eye catching rock formation known by us as La Figura, onto which Pilcaneu homestead looks.

From Pilcaniyeu, which he calls Geylum, some two hundred individuals, including Musters, made a dash northwards leaving most of the women and all the children. They were making for the place where Uncle Frank's favourite fishing river, the Caleufu, runs into the Collon Cura near where Alicura homestead now stands. Here Shaihueque, a powerful cacique, had his toldería, and it was here that the Tehuelches hoped to trade their guanaco mantles and ostrich feathers. Musters refers to the place as Las Manzanas and to the people who lived there as Manzaneros.

One evening in April 1870 Musters and a few others, the head of a straggling column, stood on a ridge looking down on the river Limay. The view was, is, tremendous. To one side the Cordillera, to the other the wide, eroded valley of the Collon Cura running from north to south, between them a pampa cut by the valleys of rivers running from the mountains. Most conspicuous is the straight gash of the Caleufu; Alicura homestead would stand one day in a gentler valley to one side. The evening was clear and they saw the lovely cone of Lanin to the north, its snow touched with pink by the setting sun. As they looked down on the river at their feet Musters' companions raised their hands to their foreheads in salute.

Shaihueque was an Araucano, a powerful cacique, clever and politically astute. Neither the Araucanos, most of whom were on bad terms with him, nor the Tehuelches of Musters' party felt safe so far inside his territory. They forded the Limay at a place where two islands stemmed the force of the current. They got safely across and, soaking wet, were warmed and fed at the fires of Incayal, a cacique who had his toldería on the northern bank. They remained there for a day or two waiting for Casimiro.

Casimiro had been chosen to head the expedition from Isla Pavon because he had connections with both Tehuelches and Araucanos and because his upbringing by the Governor of Patagones, to whom he had been given by his mother ,an alcoholic, as an infant in exchange for a barrel of rum, gave him some understanding of European customs.

Unfortunately, though not surprisingly, Casimiro was a drunkard.

He was a clever man but unreliable; unwilling or unable to stay sober, as the responsible caciques did when alcoholic beverages were available, to keep order and break up fights. It was a bout of drinking that had kept Casimiro back on this occasion. Tired of waiting five brothers, who were also sworn brothers of Musters, went off with one of Incayal's men to gather apples. The youngest borrowed Musters' revolver. They went off promising to bring plenty of fruit to share with the party when they rejoined them before the meeting with Shaihueque.

When Casimiro appeared he was in an evil temper, as always after a drinking bout. Refusing to take advantage of the fine weather he insisted on staying by the Limay for yet another day. It was pouring with rain when finally they left Incayal's tolderia and climbed up onto the Pampa Alicura. They crossed it and followed a cañadon down to the valley of the Caleufu a few kilometres above Shaihueque's tolderia.

They had stopped to make a fire and warm themselves when a rider dashed up. It was the youngest of the brothers who had gone to gather apples. He was splashed with blood and his face showed the effects of drink and violent exertion. Meeting a group of Shaihueque's men who had with them a supply of aguadiente they had started drinking together. Drink led to argument and a full scale fight. Leaving his brothers for dead the youngest had escaped after shooting several men with the revolver Musters had lent him. Uncertain of their welcome as they already were this incident created great tension. Men were sent to the scene of the fight to get the bodies and found that, though fearfully slashed, none of the brothers was dead. Three of Shaihueque's men had been killed.

As the news spread Musters and his party were joined by a number of lesser caciques, among them Incayal, anxious to pay off old scores against their powerful neighbour. The Tehuelches were against a battle which would bring to nothing the trade and discussions for which they had travelled so far. Shaihueque's attitude was not agressive; he sent an old woman who orated on the advantage of a peaceful settlement. They did not feel sure of his intentions and spent a miserable night in their camp among the clumps of pampas grass shivering round the fires and making 'bolas perdidas' (boleadoras consisting of a single stone on a rawhide thong) in preparation for a battle.

When two parties of indians met it was customary for the men to form in opposing lines and make warlike manoevres which did not come to anything if the intentions on both sides were pacific. At dawn Musters and his companions prepared their best horses and their smartest gear and rode towards the tolderia. Standing on the spot it is not difficult to picture them riding, six abreast, guns and spears in their hands, as the sun rose over the hard, straight edge of the valley, their horses, lively with morning freshness and the excitement imparted by their riders, prancing over the sandy soil with its scant covering of bushes.

About ninety of Shaihueque's men were manoevring in four groups on a piece of level ground. They were a fine sight, Musters tells us, with their bright ponchos and their spears, as they wheeled and formed keeping their distances in a way that would have done credit to regular cavalry. The Tehuelche group were right in suspecting that Shaihueque had more men concealed near by. They themselves revealed their full strength as they waited to start the ceremony of meeting. Excitement mounted. When the order was given and they raced towards the opposing line of warriors it seemed that nothing could prevent a battle. But the caciques had decided for peace. Riding ahead of their men they wheeled as the lines closed and kept them apart.

Musters with his light coloured hair and beard —which the Indians tried to persuade him to pull out hair by hair as they did all facial hair—painted and wearing a guanaco skin mantle, charged with his companions as he would have fought with them had it come to that. Many years later he tried to cross from Chile into Argentina in that latitude. He was recognised by a Manzanero as the man whose revolver had killed several of his tribe. He was taken prisoner and was lucky to get back to Chile alive.

At the time Musters was well received by Shaihueque. The Tehuelches did good trade, exchanging their guanaco skin rugs for horses and woven ponchos, and set off back to Geylum after several days of feasting and general drunkeness. Shaihueque offered to send Musters straight across the continent to the Argentine provinces, his safety guaranteed. He refused, not wishing to break faith with his Tehuelche friends, and was warmly invited to return.

The journey from Geylum eastwards across the continent to Carmen de Patagones on the Atlantic coast, was downhill in every sense. When they rejoined the party in Geylum, Pilcaniyeu as it is today, they found them suffering from a flu like sickness. They moved on hoping to leave the sickness behind leaving Geylum on the 17th of April 1870, a year to the day since Musters left the Malvinas Islands. Most of the Indians caught the sickness as did Musters; half the children died. The women lamented through the nights so that it was hard to sleep. Food was scarce as the men were often too weak to hunt. Musters arrived in Patagones in May 1870. Of the 18 Tehuelche men who had set out with their families from Isla Pavon only eight survived to reach Patagones.

Much has been said, with truth, about the terrible treatment of the indigenous peoples of South America by Europeans. Since reading Musters' book I have sometimes wondered if anything could be more cruel than the life the Indians led in their natural state. The cacique Crime pushed onto his horse to travel all day in great pain, later jolted along in a sort of stretcher between two riders, day after day for weeks until he died. Children wiped out in epidemics, the sudden jealousies and killings, the cold, the fear and the hunger.

The sort of man that Musters was and the reason he did not lose his life on his incredible journey 'with the Patagonians', can be found in the advice he gives to possible future travellers at the end of a chapter on the manners and customs of the Tehuelches.

'Never,' he writes, 'show distrust of the Indians; be as free with your goods and chattels as they are to each other. Dont ever want anything done for you: always catch your own horse. Dont give yourself ideas of superiority as they dont understand it —unless you can prove yourself better in some distinct way. Always be first, as you are not likely to be encumbered with wife or gear, in crossing rivers or any other difficulties; they will learn by degrees to respect you; in a word, as you treat them so will they treat you.'

It seems that a lot of Patagonian attitudes were learned from the indigenous peoples whose blood and spirit live on among us.

From Patagones Musters took ship to Buenos Aires where he arrived in August 1870. He cannot have stayed long because in December of that year he read a paper before the Royal Geographical Society in London. In June 1871 he retired from the Royal Navy with the rank of captain and in that same year the first edition of his book was published.

For months he was unable to sleep under a roof.

Chapter Twelve

A Camaruco

The vegetable garden in Leleque was as big, as sunny and sheltered as the one in Maiten, but the gardener I inherited did not compare to dear old Cruz, the gardener I found in Maiten. He was a tall, thin man who never took off the black beret that he wore, the 'boina vasca'. One day it was knocked off and I was surprised to see that he had a distinguished head of thick, grey hair.

He lived with his wife and five or six children in one of the cottages down the road. I asked his wife to do the washing for our house. She was the only really bad washerwoman I ever had; she could not learn to iron. There was a sort of heavy stupidity about her and all but two of the children were at the bottom of their classes at school. At the time I supposed they lacked intelligence. Looking back I wonder if this man so subservient, almost servile, in his manner to me was not a tyrant in his home and beat up his family. He was not a good gardener, though how bad I did not realise until, after a few years, he left and I took over the vegetable garden. His wife left him not long after.

To the right of the oval lawn infront of the house the path to the vegetable garden led off beneath a row of towering silver poplars. To one side of the path was a garden shed and on the other a wooden box in which we kept rakes, spades, hoes and forks. These things were gold to country people and had to be watched. What we had to lend round the estancia and seldom returned were scythes. In the end I bought my own and refused to lend it. A scythe was essential to cut back the grass at certain times of the year.

The vegetable garden was a place of sunshine and peace protected by rows of Lombardy poplars from the westerly gales that roared down off the Sta Rosa in spring and summer. A canal ran along the far end between two rows of poplars. On one side of a broad central path were lines of currant and gooseberry bushes and raspberry canes; on the other rows of the usual garden vegetables, turnips, carrots, peas, cabbages, broad beans, Swiss chard...... There was a row of seed boxes, a rather useless greenhouse that did not get enough sun and a strawberry cage. The berries ripened for Christmas and the New Year.

After my first gardener left we increased the number and variety of vegetables and lengthened the season of productivity. By 1980 when Charlie retired and we left Leleque, we had vegetables all the year round. There was not much variety in winter. Carrots buried under sand to protect them from the frost, were edible until November when the first lettuces were ready to eat. In December radishes, broad beans and spinach came on the menu. Endive, which I discovered only a few years before we left Leleque, was a joy. Sown in summer, dug up in autumn, the leaves cut off and the roots buried in sand in some old wooden seed boxes, they produced delicious, tender sprouts in June and July. It was luxury to eat a fresh salad in the middle of winter.

I had numbers of gardeners, some more some less hard working, all suffering from the non-appearance on Monday syndrome, until Floriano Nahuelquir appeared. The majority of the men who worked on Leleque came from Cushamen, anything up to a six hour ride from Leleque homestead depending on the part of the reservation they lived on. Floriano was related to the cacique. He was intelligent and used his head. He knew something about growing vegetables, was careful with the garden implements and good at figures, always arriving at the answer to questions requiring mental arithmetic, such as how many onion seedlings were required,—though too polite to admit it—before I did.

He was an excellent gardener and took pride in his work. No need to remind him to hoe or to irrigate. In autumn the garden was covered with a layer of manure that was left to lie through the winter and dug in in the spring. There was a race for manure by the owners of the various gardens on the homestead in autumn. The best was the sheep manure that fell through the slatted floor of the shearing shed, but this was the perquisite of the manager's wife. For the last ten years of our time in Leleque Charlie was General Manager. Floriano kept his eyes open, took the horse and cart some day when they were not in use, and went off to a pile he had marked down. After a year I left the vegetable garden entirely to him merely standing in when he was away.

One day I asked Floriano a question that had always puzzled me. What religion did his people profess? Nominally, of course, they were Roman Catholics but there were few priests and fewer churches in that part of the world in those days.

"The camaruco," he answered.

At the time I did not understand what he meant. I had heard of this ceremony as a sort of rain dance. It took place in autumn, a dry season, in lonely places where the population was largely indigenous.

Ester who worked in the house in our last years in Leleque was related to Floriano. She was tiny, tiny and friendly, greeting any guest who came to the house as if they were hers. Her father was brother to the cacique. We were fond of her and she of us, but she missed her family and spent a lot of her spare time writing to them. When the time of the camaruco in Cushamen came round she grew restless and upset. Unfortunately autumn was a busy time in the house; I could not spare her for the week or ten days it would take her to get to the camaruco and come back. The actual gathering might last two or three days.

One day when the camaruco was taking place and poor Ester was very low, Charlie electified us by saying that we would take her to it. Joan, who was with us, and I were hardly less delighted than Ester. We had to take a roundabout road through El Maiten where there was a bridge over the river Chubut. It was over two hours after leaving Leleque when we stopped outside the house of a family of Middle Eastern origin with whom Charlie had some business, a few kilometres from the hollow in which the camaruco was being held. We were warmly invited to lunch; they found it hard to believe that we preferred to go to the camaruco

The Cordillera was wearing its autumn colours of pale gold, dry green and various shades of brown. To the west of the hollow, above rounded hills rose the dark outlines of higher mountains; to the south west an opening showed a wide valley golden with dried grasses through which the river Chubut drew a wandering green thread. Beyond, far away on the sky line, was the blue line of the Sta Rosa.

On the level bottom of the hollow, wheel to high wheel, their lowered shafts pointing outwards, between twenty and thirty bullock carts were drawn up in a semi-circle open to the east. Among and beneath them children played and woman sat or bent over cooking pots set over fires made in pits in the ground. Horses and bullocks grazed on the enclosing slopes. The hum and babble of the four hundred odd people gathered in the hollow was absorbed into space; from time to time a laugh, a baby's cry or the neigh of a horse broke through the constant rustle of the wind.

Infront of the bullock carts, central to the whole scene, a double row of canes was planted in the ground. Among them tins and white plastic containers held modai, wheat that had been boiled and allowed to ferment. Blue and white flags flew from the two central canes and the Argentine colours were repeated in ribbons on the others. Behind the canes, two at either side, were instruments made from two metre lengths of cane, split at one end to allow the point of a horn to be inserted and then bound together again with rawhide. The mouth pieces of these "trutrucas' lay waist-high in the forks of green branches that had been stuck into the ground.

Infront of the canes, facing east away from the carts, two girls their kerchiefed heads bowed, stood motionless. Some ten metres ahead of them two boys also faced east. These four 'pehuenches', two virgins of either sex, and a white and a chestnut horse tethered near them, were the most important figures in the ritual of the camaruco . The white horse's coat was stained blue and purple, the quarters of the chestnut were sticky with modai.

It was the second and last day of a camaruco that had begun in the darkness before dawn the day before when the deep, hoarse notes of the trutrucas had called the families camped on the hills around to the ceremonial preparation of the white and chestnut horses. Outsiders were allowed, though not welcome, at this camaruco; there were one or two others besides ourselves. One of these was a Roman Catholic priest who explained to us the meaning of the various rituals. He was very insistant on the religious significance underlying them –the appeal to a higher spirit. He grew angry when he told us that under Peron's government Peron's photograph had been fixed to the canes that, in the priest's mind corresponded to the altar.

As the dusty hours passed orders shouted in Araucano by the 'cabecillo', the cacique in charge, regulated each stage of the leisurely proceedings. Now it was the turn of the boys to return thanks for health, for parents, for life. They ran into the centre infront of the canes and knelt in a row facing east. The tins of modai they carried glinted in the sun as they leapt into the air with a shout waving their arms above their heads. One little chap was late. He ran after the others, knelt and sprang like a jack-in-the-box all on his own to a murmur of laughter from the men and women watching.

The uncouth notes of the trutrucas began to sound and two men, hand in hand, moving with a rythmical step, began to circle the canes clockwise. Behind them came the male pehuenches, lads of fifteen or so who wore across their chests strips of hand woven material sown with bells; behind them again, in pairs holding hands or either end of a rebenque or poncho, men, boys and tiny children joined in. Some blew pifilcas, a sort of whistle made from a section of the stem of a dry hemlock or from a guanaco bone.

Between the canes and the men the women, using the same step circled in the opposite direction behind the female pehuenches. Directly behind the pehuenches were a pair of old women one of whom carried a small drum which she beat at intervals with a short, thick stick. Every half hour or so, at a shout from the cabecillo, the men dropped into an easy walk while the pehuenches ladled modai into a shell which they handed to the old women who took a mouthful. Before long the dance started up again, boots, shoes, alpargatas moving rythmically in the dust to the sound of pifilcas, trutrucas, jingling bells and the moaning chant of a group of women.

The last part of the camaruco began in the late afternoon when a guttural shout sent the men to prepare their horses. Some rode fat, powerful animals that held their heads proudly in bridles decorated with silver coins; some used broad martingales cut into intricate patterns or had silver ornaments hanging between the reins, carefully selected skins covering their broad recados. Others rode runtish ponies with skimpy bridles, a few shabby clothes thrown over their backs. None were rich but some were very poor.

By sunset the hollow must be empty of people. The bullock carts had been loaded with bedding rolls, pots, asadores, tins of modai and any left-over food and firewood before, at another order, the men mounted and formed two bands facing each other infront of the canes. Two or three men from either band, sitting their horses a little ahead of the others, made orations in Araucano or Mapuche using set phrases learned by heart as the language is no longer in common use.

As each orator finished he was aclaimed with high shouts. The canes were taken up and distributed among the riders together with the trutrucas and the props that supported them. The pehuenches mounted the white and chestnut horses which had been chosen for their steadiness since even a stumble would mean bad luck; a buck or a shy would be a calamity. Carrying the flags they led some two hundred horsemen at a controlled gallop in a wide circle anti-clockwise, the women dancing in the centre. The slanting rays of the sun shone on the flying flags, the procession of galloping horsemen, the blowing dust and the stoney hillsides behind. When they had completed three rounds the pehuenches led off to one side. The old woman with the drum struck three distinct notes, lifted her hands to the hills and dropped them with finality.

By nightfall the hollow would be empty. Only tracks on the ground would remain to show where a simple, rural people had enacted rituals handed down, some say, from before the Inca Empire was established.

Chapter Thirteen

Spring on the Farm

In Leleque, as on all farms, the year inside and outside the house moved to the rhythm of the farm work. June, July and August, the winter months, were quiet and cold with little movement of people or work. Towards the end of July the teros came back, the saying was that they came with last snowfall of the winter. Their loud teu teu was a sign that the darkest days were over.

August was full of promises. Daffodil shoots pushing through the cold earth, green shoots on gooseberry bushes, little brown leaves and pinking buds on a japonica that grew against a warm, north facing wall. The lilac bushes prepared little piles of purple buds, those away from the protection of a wall only realised their scented beauty once in ten years. On the 42nd parallel, seven hundred metres above sea level, a September or October without four or five degree frosts was rare. The cherry tree that shaded our asados, the apple trees in the orchard, flowered abundantly but only fruited once every five or six years. Pears did better. It was the height rather than the latitude that was to blame. In the mountain valleys farther west, in Epuyen and El Bolson three and four hundred metres lower, trees and bushes flowered three weeks earlier and fruited normally.

The month of September was touched with gold and green in the protected areas round the house though the open countryside still wore a dull winter look. In September daffodils and dandelions flowered; birds that had spent the winter in warmer climes started coming back. In ground that had been worked, or in loose, sandy soil by the stream dandelion roots sent hanks of pale, unformed leaves to the surface. If found when just the tips were showing they made a good salad; it was a joy to eat something green at that time of the year. The sheep loved to eat the flowers and walked around with yellow powdered noses. For many years the first daffodil opened on September 17th in full view of the galería windows.

In September lambing began. The fields across the road where the stud ewes lambed under Don Ricardo's watchful eye, were full of lambs, toddling, running, dancing, collecting in bands to play. The ewes grazed quietly until one or another in sudden alarm hurried to the lambs calling and sniffing, searching for her own. There were plenty of birds by then but September is a windy month and they kept low among the bushes and clumps of tussock grass. Spring on the 42nd parallel, seven hundred metres above sea level, was the usual farmer's mix of joy and frustration.

In early November when the osier willows that marked the lines of the streams were in pale, new leaf, when hills and mountains were smokey blue or faintly green, when watercourses ran high with melting snow, birds nested and wild flowers began their brief flowering, the lambs were ready to be marked.

The day the lamb marking gang left the homestead to start work was a landmark on the farm calendar. We all went to see them set out. First there was a procession of four carts each pulled by three fat, excited cart horses, under exercised since the farm had been partly mechanised. They were accompanied by about eight riders and a troop of spare horses. Two of the carts were loaded with nets, wooden sections and iron stakes for making temporary yards, another carried rations for ten days and firewood, the fourth was piled with bedding rolls. Last came the Veinte carrying the appurtanences of the mayor domo in charge of the lamb marking, the estancia manager's second in command.

The Veinte was a light, four wheeled vehicle that had been No 20 in the mule train that provisioned the estancias before roads and railways came to Patagonia. Adapted to horse traction it had been used by general managers on their tours of the Company properties; now it was brought out of retirement once a year to take part in the first stages of lamb marking when the river Chubut had to be forded. After that lorry and pick up took over.

The lamb marking gang moved from ewe flock to ewe flock marking, castrating and removing the lamb's tails. The shepherd in charge of each flock had been moving the sheep gently in a certain direction for days. They were mustered by the men in each section under their foreman as the gang was ready for them. Two large flocks or three smaller ones were marked each day. The same camping grounds which must have water, a piece of level ground on which to set up the yards and, if possible, shelter, were used year after year.

Charlie went out nearly every day to watch the progress of the gang and get the counts −the number of lambs marked in each flock. The success of the year's working depended on a good lambing. Once a year he spent a day with them and I and the family accompanied him. This was usually when the gang was working in the valley of the Chubut, about a two hour drive from the homestead.

The carts, bumping one after the other along a faint track to where the flock had been mustered, were slightly reminiscent of covered wagons in a Western. Two of them stopped. The yards were unloaded and men jumped into action, hammering stakes into the ground, unrolling nets, looping ropes. The other carts drove on to the 'campamento' where the horses were unharnessed and loosed to graze with the rest of the troop. Fires were lit, cauldrons for puchero set over them and 'asadores' with ribs of sheep threaded on them were stuck into the ground to cook slowly at some distance from the heat. The puchero, made with the backbone of a sheep cut up and boiled with plenty of water, vegetables if available, and rice or fideos, was delicious.

Meanwhile the yards had been set up. Their nerve centre was a couple of wooden pens five metres square with a side in common. On one of the long sides of the rectangle made by the pens a curved line of netting enclosed an area the shape of the final section in the diagram that children scratch on the ground for a game of hopscotch. On the opposite side a rectangular yard was closed at the far end by a pair of gates; from either end of these wings of netting extended outwards in a shallow V.

When the yards were completed the men who had been making them lay down behind the wings of netting. Horsemen who had been holding a flock of ewes and lambs set them moving slowly into the space between the rows of men lying prone and absolutely still. Once the sheep were inside the ends of the V the riders jumped off their horses and hurried them on with shouts, rebenques waving, the men who were holding the ends of the netting jumped to their feet and ran towards each other and the milling, maaing mob of sheep was enclosed.

Iron stakes were driven into the ground to hold the nets and as many sheep as possible were pushed through the gates into the rectangular yard, from which one of the small pens was filled. The ewes were looked over, vaccinated and treated, if necessary, for flyblow, before being let into the final hopscotch area.

The lambs, meanwhile, had been picked out from among the ewes and dropped into the pen next door where they were picked up again and held in a sitting position on a board fixed horizontally along the top of the pen. Three or four men with bloodstained sacking protecting their clothes stood on the other side of the board. As the lamb was moved along infront of them the first made a nick in its ear to mark its age, the next, if it was a pedigree flock, made another to indicate its breeding, the third castrated the male lambs and the fourth, with a flick of his knife, removed the tail which was thrown onto a pile that the majordomo counted later. The lamb was dropped to the ground and ran, bleeding and unhappy, to join the mob and add its voice to the chorus of ewes and lambs crying for one another.

When all the sheep had been through the yards these were dismantled and the men went to the fires to rest, drink mate and eat in the shelter of pampas grass or shrubs. Two horsemen remained with the flock while the ewes and lambs were mothering up; unless the mob was held together for at least two hours many of the lambs would never find their mothers again.

Men burned black by the sun and the wind drank mate round fires over which cauldrons of puchero boiled and ribs of sheep cooked over the embers. A knife was stuck into the back of each 'faja'; mountains shimmered at the head of the valley; horses grazed or, heads upflung, stared into distances from which came faintly the shouts of distant musterers. A carancho with its young croaked from a nest too large for the scrubby tree it burdened and, as the ewes and lambs found each other and their clamour faded a song sparrow could be heard. It was as though one had stepped back to a younger, simpler Argentina, the one Hudson and Cunningham Graham described, where Martin Fierro and Don Segundo Sombra lived.

When the lambs in the Leleque, Potrada and Fofocahuel sections had been marked, about ten days work if the weather was good, some of the gang went on to Montoso and Lepa for a further ten days. In Leleque there was about a week's pause between the end of lamb marking and the start of shearing in the second or third week of November.

The shearing was done by a gang of contract shearers run, when I first knew it, by Ramon Ituarte. When he died, sadly young, his son took over. Don Ramon was a man with an air of quiet authority. Greeting our children when they were very young he had the habit, unusual in a country where children are kissed rather than taught to shake hands, of holding out his hand and waiting patiently until they grasped what was expected of them and put the right hand in his. He ran his gang with the same mixture of patience and firmness.

The gap between the end of lamb marking and the beginning of shearing was one of suspense. Don Ramon's head-quarters were some 1000 kilometres north and east of Leleque. His gang had been shearing for over two months by the time they reached us. They might be held up by rain or any other problem, human or mechanical, that can overtake a group of about twenty men moving from farm to farm in sparsely populated country over a period of months. If they arrived over a week late it was goodbye to any hope of getting finished before the fiestas.

While the shearing was on everything took second place to getting the wool off the sheep's backs. The homestead ticked over with a skeleton staff while the shearing shed, five kilometres up the valley, hummed and throbbed with activity. From the last week of November until sometime around Christmas when the last sheep, skinny without its wool, dazed by noise and handling, staggered out into the counting pen, the life of the estancia revolved around this group of buildings. They were the centre of an operation that brought flocks of sheep from all over the property (the most distant had a five day walk), and returned them shorn.

Shepherds responsible for the stock on each stretch of hill and valley were out of their cottages all day mustering and trooping. The holding paddocks by the shearing shed where the sheep waited their turn to be shorn and recuperated afterwards, grew more bare and dusty as the days passed. To keep them a little grassy the movement of the flocks had to be carefully synchronised, the flow continuous.

The original part of the shearing shed had rough, thick walls of flagstones set in mud and was used as a deposit for bales of wool and skins. The newer part of the building, which measured about 100 metres by 35 altogether, was made of galvanised iron sheeting with which the whole was roofed. On two sides of the shed there was a maze of sheep yards dotted with osier willows and sheltered by rows of poplars. Near it were three or four houses where the foreman in charge and the ten men under him lived, and where the shearers were fed and housed.

The foreman's house stood behind a hedge of elderberry. His oldest son was doing his military service with the army at the time of the Malvinas conflict in 1982. He came back safely. Being Patagonian he knew how to look after himself in the cold and the wet of the islands to which, for some strange reason, so many lads from the sub-tropical northern provinces were sent.

During shearing the yards were full of sheep,men,dogs and dust. With sheep from all over the estancia gathered there it was a good moment to do jobs like classing, taking off dry ewes and marking any lambs that had been missed out or been too young to mark earlier. Inside the shed too all was movement and activity. Up to twenty shearers worked along the walls under the overhead transmission that whirred and clattered as it carried electric current to the shears. At intervals the high note of blades being sharpened on a revolving stone penetrated the din. Men using brooms with a quick, short action swept up wool fallen on the floor and put it into tall baskets.

Woolly sheep shut in two rows of pens down the middle of the shed were caught one by one and left lying with their feet tied in the narrow space between the pens and the shearers. When a shearer opened the little door in the wall of the shed beside him and let a shorn sheep out into the counting pen, there was always another to hand. As he made the last stroke with his shears down the back legs and the fleece came away, a man gathered it up and hurried down to the end of the shearing shed where the wool classer stood behind a table. The man with the fleece flung it wide over the table and the classer and he rolled it into a big, soft ball.

The classer looked at the wool, gave a piece a tug to test its soundness and deposited the fleece in one of a row of open ended cubicles behind him. On the other side of the cubicles was the wool press where the wool was pressed into 300 kilo bales. Round the top of the press were the words; 'John Shaw and Sons. Made in Salford.' It had been installed in 1937.

If the shearing was not finished before the fiestas it seemed to go on for ever. The rythm of work once broken was hard to pick up again. Everyone was tired of the shearing. The estancia people wanted to get on to other jobs, the shearers wanted to get on to another estancia. The fiestas were spoiled. Some of our New Year parties ended at six o'clock in the morning with everyone going down to the shed to shut in sheep for the shearers who were working over New Year's day to get finished.

Chapter Fourteen

Summertime

The summer months, December, January and Febuary were active and social. Our daughters were on holiday from school, there were family visits and sheep shows to attend; wool and stock buyers, veterinary salesmen, government officials and friends passing through would come to the house for a drink or a meal. There might be a director's visit. It was in summer that the gardens, flower and vegetable, needed most attention and it was in summer that the domestic staff, who had worked steadily through the quiet winter, were most likely to take time off, with or without advising.

The only time a Director and his wife came to spend Christmas with us in Leleque the girl who was working in the house at the time got knocked down while helping her husband tame a horse, two days before they arrived. As she was pregnant she had to take to her bed. A director being involved a car was sent to fetch a very capable girl, daughter of a shepherd, who had worked for me before so the problem was quickly solved. Just a typical summer crisis.

Apart from regular visitors there was a flow of odd characters, as well as the young and moneyless looking for free meals and a lodging. When in the 1960's a cloud of ramblers discovered Patagonia the custom of never refusing a lift, of slowing down to make sure that a car stopped at the roadside was not in trouble, started to disappear. Off the main roads they still applied.

When I went to live in Patagonia hospitality was a law; a tradition that had come down from days not long past when the population was sparse and not to help a fellow human in need might be to condemn him or her to death. If one had food one shared it. I learned this lesson in Patgonian manners in Maiten estancia when a dress-maker came from the town to measure our children for pyjamas. I took her into the warmest part of the house, the drawing room, to measure them. The table was laid there for tea with a cake, jams etc. It did not occur to me to invite someone I hardly knew, who was there to do a job of work, to tea. Charlie came in just as she left. He looked at the table and said,

"Did you invite her to tea? She will have expected it."

I hope this woman has forgotten my bad manners; I never have.

Some years ago a wealthy and well known European family bought the Argentine Southern Land properties. I asked a friend who worked with them for a time what he thought of them as people. After a moment's thought he said,

"I dont like their ways."

He told us how he taken several members of this family with the small son of one of them to a the cottage of a shepherd who lived on a very isolated part of the property. The shepherd was there with his wife and a troop of children.

"There was this fat boy sucking sweets all the time infront of the children and he never offered them any, nor did his father tell him to." There was all the weight of Patagonian tradition –not to mention biblical– in the scandalised tone of his voice.

Until I lived in Leleque I never realised how many people have the urge to join the northern and southernmost points of the Americas, to travel from Alaska to Tierra del Fuego or vice versa. They attempted it in every sort of vehicle or without. Leleque on a lonely stretch of the Ruta Cuarenta that runs along the Argentine side of the Andes from the frontier with Bolivia to some hundred kilometres from the Straits of Magellan, was right in their path.

The North American couple in an amphibious vehicle that broke down near Leleque were before my time. They lived in the staff house while their vehicle was being repaired; the manager's wife, a notable cook, rated a mention for her English teas in the article they wrote about their journey which was published in The Saturday Evening Post. We once had an Australian radiologist and her German husband, named Adolf, spend the night under the hawthorn trees in the drive. They had come from Alaska in a Combi.

Then there was the man who was walking it. His Japanese wife, travelling in a vehicle, arranged food and, when possible, lodging. They spent a night in the staff house. I wonder how far they got. There were several riders trying to out do Tschiffley who started his famous ride near Buenos Aires though the horses he rode, Mancha and Gato, were from Patagonia.

One summer afternoon I was in the kitchen icing a cake for Uncle Tom and his wife who were visiting Argentina and due any minute from Esquel airport, when there was a knock on the back door. Outside I found an elderly man wearing Highland dress, kilt, glengarry, thick three quarter length socks and brogues. He had an accent to match his clothes. This Scot had decided in his late fifties to go from Tierra del Fuego to Alaska on a motor bike. He shared our tea, spent a night and carried on next morning. We had a letter from, I think, Houston some months later. He had fallen ill and was in hospital there.

One afternoon an extraordinary looking vehicle came to a stop in the yard by the garages and the occupants walked up the back drive to ask if they could look round the homestead. He was a man of seventy who had once worked in Leleque; his wife was some years younger. They were pensioners who made up for lack of money with ingenuity. He had made a little house on the chassis of a Ford truck. There was a painted sign, "jubilados" under the eves of the corrugated iron roof. When they took a holiday from their tiny dairy farm in the province of Buenos Aires they travelled very slowly, very independently, about the lonely spaces of Argentina. All they would take with us was a cup of tea. They had eaten particularly well at midday, they said. Coming on a man hoeing potatoes in the valley of El Hoyo they had begged a few, cooked them then and there and had a delicious meal of new potatoes.

Another surprise visit became a long distance friendship that has lasted to this day. Charlie found this youthful looking white haired man and his charming, softly spoken wife on the homestead asking in halting Spanish if anyone had seen any bats.

"Bats!" said Charlie, "I'll show you bats." We had a plague of them in the roof of the house.

This man was a professor at Berkeley College, California, who had come to Argentina in the first place to give a course in ecology at a university in Buenos Aires. His subject was, I think, small mammals. It was fascinating to hear him talk about the development of our countryside over millions of years.

They insisted on using their own sleeping arrangements; it was difficult to persuade them into the house for so much as a cup of tea or a drink. They hung fine nets across the drive in the evening and lay sleeping bags on the verandah. In the day time they skinned any bats they had trapped in the nets and he would pin them out on boards while she took notes. We always referred to them as the Bat Hunters but the last time they came by they had discovered, I am glad to say, some utterly new and exciting kind of mouse.

Once a friend wrote to Charlie asking if a group of boys from one of the more expensive and well known boarding schools in Buenos Aires could spend a few days on the estancia as part of a Patagonian excursion that had been planned for them. Charlie went to some trouble making arrangements and having horses set aside for the boys to use.

The group of fourteen and fifteen year old lads arrived in Leleque on a day when we were in Esquel at the Sheep Show. We arrived back to find them there with the master who was supposed to be in charge. They had made themselves very much at home, wandering around the vegetable garden, picking what they fancied and telling Pola, the cook, what they wanted for supper. Pola, who did not approve of strangers telling her what to do in her own kitchen, had a very bleak look in her eye when we got back in the late evening.

The first night, as it was late, the boys were to pitch their tents by the hawthorn drive and use our front bathroom. We were tired and getting to bed early when we heard stones rattling against the glass of our curtained windows. The boys had picked the wrong one; our daughters' room was further along the wing of the house. Charlie jumped out of bed, pulled on his shirt and trousers and hurried out to tell someone what he thought of them. The master was having a bath so he went out to the tent and told the boys, hidden inside by now, what he thought of their behaviour. He said, among other things, that any paisano would know better how to return hospitality.

Our daughters were shocked at their father's language but I think the boys enjoyed it. Charlie earned a place in the poem, Hiawatha style, published in the school magazine in which they recounted their experiences on their tour of the south. One or two came back a year later having been rained out of a camp in El Bolson, and were a great addition to our New Year party.

New Year was an awkward date to celebrate as domestic staff had their own parties to attend, so we invited friends of all ages, in or outside the Company, who cared to join us in a buffet meal. Most of our guests had never heard of Old Lang Syne and joining hands in a circle, arms crossed, to sing it as we had always done on New Year's Eve at Chirú, but they took to it with enthusiasm.

One lot of summer visitors were four footed. We had noticed a slight smell of skunk in our bedroom now and then –a mild whiff of skunk is not unpleasant. Then we noticed a skunk crossing the lawn infront of the house. Finally we discovered that they had made an entrance under the verandah by the front door. They must have made a burrow under our bedroom; one day we discovered another entrance in the path that ran round the lawn in the centre of the patio at the back of the house.

One Sunday we arrived back from a day's outing to find that Mrs Skunk was moving house. Carrying her babies by the neck in her mouth she made her way round the patio, through a narrow gap under the garden door, through the back yard, across the drive and a field, over a wooden plank laid across the canal, under a gate and across the corral by the milking shed to a hole in the bank beyond, a distance of about a hundred metres. She made the journey several times.

Joan yearned for a baby skunk. With the smell glands removed they make the most attractive pets. We were never able to catch one at the right age, besides, one hesitates to tamper with nature's defenses in a wild animal. Nor were we able to get rid of them. No matter how often and how firmly the entrances to the burrow were blocked they were always unblocked when the breeding season came. Only once was the smell in our bedroom overpowering –a matrimonial disagreement perhaps, or a stranger skunk trying to take over. It was only for a month or to in the year that their Leleque residence was in use.

Sheep Shows were a summer activity, though the biggest and best
known in Argentina, if not the most prestigious among Australian
Merino sheep breeders, was the Palermo Show which took place in
July in Buenos Aires. Through the summer months there were sheep
shows in towns all down the Atlantic coast of Patagonia from
Patagones to Rio Gallegos and two or three in the interior. Leleque
stud sent rams to several of the most important and they were expected to do well.

A Show was a four day affair. The sheep had to be in the show
grounds by a certain hour on a cerain day, usually a Thursday, to be
examined by veterinarians and given a clean bill of health. Judging
took place on the Friday afternoon and Saturday. The Inauguration,
this always seemed a contradiction in terms, when speeches were made
and prizes presented was on Saturday afternoon or Sunday. Most important and nerve wracking of all were the sales on Monday. The sheep
were sold by auction and the Judge's decisions proved right or wrong
in the eyes of the average farmer by the price he was willing to pay for
the animals selected. Occasionally a Grand Champion would sell for
less than a ram that had been passed over in the judging. The name of
the stud by which the sheep was presented also affected the price. A
good name for the health nd performance of the rams it produced
was sometimes enough to ensure a good price.

To the time a show lasted had to be added the time it took to get
there and back. Comodoro Rivadavia, where the biggest and most
important of the southern sheep shows took place, was a day's drive
away, as was the Viedma Show on the banks of the Rio Negro opposite Patagones. Esquel was just over an hour's run from Leleque. A
centre for Australian Merino sheep breeders Esquel was also a centre
of the Welsh Colony in Chubut. It was worth going to the Show just
to hear them sing the National Anthem.

Shows were a pleasant break in farm routine; our stay paid in a good hotel; meeting old friends and making new ones; going out to meals and parties. When our children were small they were also exhausting, going to bed late and getting up at the usual time.

The show shed in Comodoro Rivadavia was enormous. The sanded space in the centre where the judges worked was conveniently situated by the bar. While the judges did their job, opening up the sheep's wool, looking at their teeth and horns, making them stand and walk, the rest of us sat at the tables or stood by the bar, gossiping or watching according to our interests and inclinations. There was never a lack of small children playing in the sand round the edge of the ring under the noses of the sheep and the feet of the judges. Their older brothers and sisters raced round in packs among the sheep pens and stands that sold anything from veterinary products to launches, leather goods or drawings.

Comodoro Rivadavia, a wealthy city surrounded by oil wells, was crowded between a steep hill and the sea; much of it was on a slope. The show grounds were on a sort of ramp, a level space extended out from a hillside which had been cut away to make space for the shed. Comodoro is not a pretty place, little could be persuaded to grow in those coastal cities; the wind was fierce and continuous even by Patagonian standards. At the Inauguration one would sit, dressed in one's best, listening to speeches in a cloud of dust shaken from the roof of the shed by a 90 kilometre gale.

There is a colony of Boer families in the area. I have an idea that they left South Africa after the Boer War to settle on the other side of the Atlantic, sometime at the start of this century. A number of us were sitting by the bar watching the judging when there was a fearful crash and a cloud of dust rose from a corner of the shed beyond the pens. Everyone disappeared, either away from the dust or towards it.

When it cleared an elderly man of Boer descent and I were the only ones left by the bar. I went over to him and asked what he thought had happened.

"Do you think it was a bomb?"

"No, no, not a bomb," he answered as we gazed at a jagged hole in the roof. "A tube of gas exploded."

We were both wrong. The brakes on a truck loaded with gravel had failed as it made its way down the hill-side above the Show Shed. The driver had jumped clear; the truck ran on and crashed through the roof of the Shed, ending up in the opposite corner. By some kindly intervention of fate the flocks of children were in some other part of the shed. No one was killed or seriously injured so the roof was patched up and the Show went on.

In those days the Palermo Show began on or about the 20th of July, during the winter holidays from school. It was a huge affair where every breed of cattle and horse was shown as well as sheep, pigs, rabbits, turkeys, hens, every kind of domestic animal or bird. The sheep section was not very large, particularly as regards Australian Merinos. For the first week the grounds were pleasantly quiet, a good place for children; as the days passed they became more and more crowded. For the week-end of the Inauguration and the official opening of the Show by the President of Argentina most country people kept away.

Leleque stud won a medal in recognition of having won the prize for the best fleece presented at the Palermo Show for ten years running. The medal was presented by the Banco de la Nación. José Martinez de Hoz, president of the bank at that time presented it and Charlie representing the Argentine Southern Land Company received it.

Chapter Fifteen

Autumn

By the end of February the lawns around the house were dry in places. The roses were over, phlox scented the air and a hollyhock might loll its head through the bathroom window, the flowers at the top of the stem reminding us that summer was coming to an end.

The air on the homestead was filled with dust, the grind of heavy vehicles and the high yelps of men driving sheep. The dirt roads had a blank look, the tracks of tires wiped out by an all over pattern of little hoof marks. In November and December buyers came to pick cattle, sheep and horses; cars whose number plates showed that they had come from the provinces of Neuquen, Rio Negro, La Pampa, or Sta Cruz as well as, of course, Chubut, stood by the butcher's shop where a clump of poplars made a patch of shade, or outside the store with its low roof, wooden sign and small, barred windows. In February and March the animals were loaded onto trucks or pick ups and taken away, lightening off the estancia and saving precious feed for the winter months.

The end of February was mushroom time. There is something magical about mushrooms. Almost everyone loves to gather them. Children who have to be driven or bribed to collect strawberries even though they are going to eat them later, love to go mushrooming. In Leleque we might find mushrooms in the level fields round the homestead as early as February and as late as June.

The single, double and triple rows of poplars that criss-crossed the homestead began to change colour in March. By early April, if the weather was frosty and still they were a golden yellow that intensified the blue or grey of the sky and the misty shades of the mountains. When the leaves began to fall the ground beneath became yellow too. I remember April sunsets when the poplar lined back drive was a passage way carpeted and walled with gold leading into a golden sky.

In a good mushroom season there was no golden climax to the year. A mushroom year was mild and damp. Provided that the ground was not too cold by the time it rained —summer was a dry season- mushrooms might appear. They popped up overnight, round buttons or fat umbrellas, white above, a soft, pleated pink beneath that ran through light and dark brown to black as they grew older.

They favoured certain places. Some years there were none, other years an afternoon's walking would yield just enough for a dish of mushrooms. Perhaps once in ten years, perhaps for three years running we would have a warm, wet autumn and for a week or ten days there would be mushrooms everywhere, growing singly, in groups or fairy circles, between thistles, among the rubbery stems of onion grass or shining white in grassy spaces.

There was another type of mushroom that appeared under pine trees of a certain variety. They were sticky brown above and yellow sponge beneath. They were much larger than the field mushrooms; peeling them was a messy business. Cleaning and peeling mushrooms is a family job best done at a table in the kitchen or on the floor with a small knife for cutting off the earthy tip of the stalk, a damp cloth for wiping fingers, a sheet of newspaper for rubbish and another for the peeled mushrooms. Any that are too dry, sodden or fly struck are best left in the fields to augment the next year's harvest.

Of the sound mushrooms we put the smallest aside to be boiled a few minutes in vinegar and water, then packed into jars with slices of garlic and a bay leaf before being covered with oil. We dried by far the greatest number; though nothing is more delicious than fresh mushrooms fried in butter only the strongest stomachs can stand them day after day.

Magic is for enchanted evenings and autumn afternoons when poplar trees stand like flames and the ancient presence of the mountains adds beauty and significance to the passing moment. It is not for everyday. When mushrooms hung in strings over all the heaters and covered every available space, when the kitchen smelled of vinegar and I had run out of paper bags for storing the dried ones, I groaned to see yet another basketful carried into the kitchen. By next the next autumn that was forgotten and as the days started to shorten we hurried out, basket in hand, as egerly as ever.

February was the last month of the summer holidays. Our daughters usually did a bit of fire fighting before they went back to school. It seldom rained during the summer months and as the hills grew dry, the water level dropped and rivers and lakes shrank, the fire risk became greater. There were forest fires in the Cordillera and grass fires further east.

After a hot summer following a mild winter and dry spring one felt that one was living on a box of matches that might flare up at any moment. A lighted cigarette butt, a spark or even a piece of glass that concentrated the sun's rays was all that was needed to set the dry, seeded grasses alight. The passing of the trencito, such a cheering sight in general or when the ground was covered in snow, roused very different feelings at these times. The clinkers it sometimes dropped were the worst fire risk of all.

Sunday was a bad day for a fire. There were always people on the homestead on a week day. When a fire was reported the siren that marked the beginning and end of work periods sounded, messages ran hither and thither and within fifteen or twenty minutes a pick up set off with men and spades, other vehicles following as people collected. A fire was an emergency. Everyone, office worker, milkman, manager and assistants hurried to the shed where spades were handed out and a vehicle waited.

Although it is exhausting to walk across rough, prickly hills throwing earth on flames most of the men, the younger ones especially, enjoyed the break in routine, the hand to hand fight, the sense of common purpose, foreman, manager and peon sweating side by side. Charlie, worried about fences and grass for the stock could not actually enjoy a fire, but even he was glad to get out of the office, returning hours later scratched and blistered, his face blackened and his socks full of burrs, too tired and thirsty to worry about anything .

Even a grass fire in the pre-Cordillera might start up again after it appeared to be extinguished if wind or hot sun brought to life embers at the heart of a pile of horse droppings or a neneo bush, outwardly cold and black. In the thick woods of the Cordillera proper only a good rain put out a fire —wisps of smoke rose from ravines and slopes within the burnt area for weeks after the main fires had been extinguished.

It is dreadful to see a forest fire burning over hills and up mountains, consuming their green and varied covering, making their hidden glades and shady streams ugly and bare. Its appetite is capricious; a stately grove of coihues stands intact on a desolate hillside, one ciprés among five hundred scorched and blackened trees is green and perfect. After watching destruction on this scale every insignificant bush, every leaf on it, seems precious.

One year forest fires scarred the mountains and filled the air with smoke day after day through January and February. Slopes above El Bolson, near Epuyen and into the mountains from Esquel, to mention a few of the nearer ones, would carry the white skeletons of trees standing above the new growth for at least fifty years.

The fire near Epuyen started one Saturday at midday when a fire lit to cook an asado got out of control. By Thursday it had been reduced to one front burning along a mountainside, threatening a range of wooded slopes. Men in the employ of Vialidad Provincial, working their huge machines at dangerous angles on the steep slopes, made a fire break from the road at the foot of the range to the bare rocks at the top. Tired fire fighters, smothered in smoke, held the lines of the road and the fire break through Thursday night while a strong wind carried burning rubbish over them, until early on Friday when rain, the first in three months, damped down the flames and they were brought under control.

Some weeks later the driver of a road machine making fire breaks ahead of a fire in the mountains west of Esquel was killed when he got too near the edge of a precipice and the machine went over.

Chapter Sixteen
Don Ricardo's Funeral

Pedro Butazzi, Pedro Gonzalez and Ricardo Courteney were senior members of the Leleque community. All had spent the greater part of their working lives with the Argentine Southern Land Company.

Pedro Butazzi, who was our Father Christmas, was in charge of the Leleque store. He was a tough old-timer whose hair had been red before it turned grey. As a young man he drove a lorry in the days before the roads were graded, when they followed tracks originally used by the Indians and later marked by bullock carts and mule trains. Some slopes were very steep indeed.

It was one of these north of Pilcaneu that Pedro tackled one day in his lorry. It came to a stop half way up so he backed down and took the hill at speed. This time he got further up but still not to the top. Down he backed again, right back, and came at the slope with every bit of speed the engine could produce. Still the lorry did not get to the top. In a fury Pedro jumped out and fired three shots into the engine.

All his children had red hair though not all were quick tempered. There was a football ground on a grassy stretch in front of the row of foremen's cottages in Leleque. Two or three times a summer teams would come from Epuyen, El Bolson or Gualjaina to play or our team would go to them. We could not do much against teams from the bigger towns but we did sometimes beat Epuyen. The first game of football I watched in Patagonia was in Epuyen at the head of its winding lake. My attention was distracted from the game by the magnificent scenery against which the ball curved in its flight and by the alpargatas that now and then soared after it.

The Leleque team's most successful year was the year we had painters working on the homestead. A small fair lad with an angel face and a quick temper, who spent his working hours balanced on the top of a high ladder brush in hand, was a particularly good footballer and carried the team to heights never reached before or after.

Once the older generation were so rash as to abandon the comfortable position of arm chair critic and took the field for half a period to show their juniors how the game should be played. For the first twenty minutes they flipped the ball about in a very fancy style, then they slowed down, and down...... and down..... All except Pedro who kept running to the end.

I remember being particularly grateful to his daughter, a straight forward, outspoken young woman, red haired of course, who was married to the man in charge of Leleque post office and captain of the football team. A team came to play bringing a pink shirted referee who blatantly favoured his own side. Pedro's daughter got out of the car in which she was sitting, sat on the bonnet and told him in clear, carrying tones what we all thought of him.

Pedro González was in charge of the bulls, stallions and brood mares. He was tall and angular. It was quite something to see him dance the cueca at an estancia celebration; poncho swirling, boots stamping, an Argentine Don Quijote. It was also good to see him concentrated on the job. The foals were brought in with their mothers every so often during the summer to be handled so that when the time came for them to be tamed they were already accustomed to humans and to handling. There was not the cruel shock of the 'doma'. Animals trusted Don Pedro and so did children. When our daughters went back to school they always took the horses they rode to him and went off secure that they would be looked after.

Don Ricardo, Dick as he was sometimes called, was in charge of the pedigree ewe flocks. He and his wife, Mercedes, lived in the last cottage of the row, the farthest from the road. The wife of a previous manager told me how Don Ricardo had come to the Manager's house one evening, boots shining, a handsome poncho over a clean, white shirt, and rung the front door bell. Most people came to the back door which was closest to the rest of the farm. He had come to ask for the hand of the stout person I knew as Doña Mercedes, his wife, then a pretty girl working in the Manager's house. She had no relations at hand so he came to speak to her boss with all the formality that struck him as appropriate to the occasion and was received in the same way.

Twice a day at the sound of the siren the slight figure, head carried forward, back erect, would walk the length of the row of cottages, cross the main road and take the one that led off to the stables. There he would saddle up, Don Ricardo's horses were quiet and gentle like himself, and ride out to the fields where the stud ewes pastured.

While he was waiting for the bus at the stop on the road by the police station one day , he had a heart attack. He was dead by the time they got him to the doctor in El Maiten.

Don Ricardo's body was waked all that night in the front room of his cottage. 'Acompañando' it was called; keeping the dead person and his family company at that sad moment. Someone would come in at the door, stand by the coffin in the centre of the room, look long and seriously at the face of the dead man or woman, then take a chair by the wall, talking in a low voice, or not at all. It was all very natural and simple.

The next day, a grey day in early spring, every adult on the property who could get there gathered outside the cottage. Vehicles were sent to the more distant sections to bring them. There were fifty or sixty individuals, mostly men with weathered faces and opaque, dark eyes, wearing open necked shirts and bombachas tucked into boots. The hills at the head of the valley were misty grey, the trees round the cottage, the row of poplars on the far side f the football ground were leafless and black with rain.

Six elderly men carried the coffin out of the door of the cottage, manoeuvred it with difficulty through the garden gate and turned into the open, grassy stretch that led to the road. The procession formed. At its head was Pedro Butazzi carrying a plain, newly made cross. Then came the highly polished coffin carried by a succession of pall bearers, eager hands grabbing for the heavy, silvered handles before those who held them wished to let go. Behind the coffin walked Don Ricardo's family, the sturdy, black clad figure of Doña Mercedes with a sturdy, black clad sister on either side, her tall sons and weeping daughter behind. The rest of us followed.

Pedro led us past the cottages, over the road and across the big yard surrounded by workshops and garages where where the blacksmith, carpenters and mechanics worked, soldering and welding, overhauling carts, wheel barrows, cars, trucks and tractors, mending gates and attending to all the other repairs and renewals necessary on a farm far from a town. All was quiet and deserted; everyone was keeping Don Ricardo company today.

A splutter of rain fell as we passed from the comparative shelter of the buildings into a poplar lined field where uncut firewood was piled in heaps and rows —a two year supply for the stoves and fireplaces of Leleque. We passed through a gate in the fence by the railway and climbed the embankment. To one side the shining rails of the narrow gauge railway ran straight to the road before curving out of sight among irrigated fields and the rows of poplars that protected them, to the other the fence on either side of the track narrowed to the steel girders of a bridge. From the station, five kilometres distant, came the faint whistle of an engine.

"I hope the last person through remembers to shut the gate," Charlie murmured beside me as we walked down the far side of the embankment.

The path was now almost hidden by long, wet grass. The men carrying the coffin teetered as they crossed a watercourse bridged by unsteady logs. They passed a wood and came onto firmer ground. The crosses of the little graveyard came into sight at the summit of a slope. Charlie, who wanted to carry his old friend the last step of his way, stepped forward and took one of the handles of the coffin but had to give way to some importunate young man before they reached the top of the slope.

The graveyard was open to the wind and to the mountains whose mighty presence was obscured by clouds that rested on the rocky summits, hung veils along the upper slopes and lay in long swathes farther down. The coffin was set down beside the open grave, looped with ropes and lowered. There was no priest to say a prayer or read a service. Doña Mercedes, followed by her family, Ricardo's old friends and everyone from Charlie to the humblest peón, stepped forward to throw a handful of earth into the grave.

Then, one man taking over from another as he grew tired, they took spades and started to fill the grave. The cross was put in position and secured with earth. Once the grave was filled and the surface most tenderly and carefully smoothed those of us who had brought flowers laid them on it; jam jars with daffodils and primulas were stood about it. It only remained for candles to be pressed into the earth and lit.

We were standing a little retired from the grave, Charlie talking to a stout, smooth skinned foreman from an outlying section when, under the murmur of their voices I heard another sound. Emerging from the trees on the other side of the road was an engine pulling a string of wagons. It chuffed round a curve, crossed the road and started along the straight that led past the graveyard to the bridge. A grey pony grazing within the fenced off area by the railway lifted its head, stared at the engine, took fright and started to canter along beside the embankment away from it.

"They didn't shut the gate," said Charlie, his eyes following mine. "The poor devil hasn't a chance."

The pony, his head held high to avoid a trailing halter rope, galloped on faster and faster to where the fences narrowed to the bridge. Every eye except those of Don Ricardo's immediate family was on it in its desperate race. It had swerved onto the embankment and was racing by the rails some twenty yards ahead of the whistling engine when they passed out of sight behind a wood that concealed the bridge from the graveyard.

I closed my eyes and prayed. "Not here. Not at **your** funeral Ricardo."

When I opened them people were leaving, trailing in one's and two's down the slope from the graveyard. Some of the younger boys had reached the railway and, in reaction to the long solemnity of wake and funeral, went running and bounding along it towards the bridge.

They found the grey pony grazing by the stream. He had jumped the fence, breaking the top wire, and fallen two metres to the edge of the water. There was hardly a scratch on him.

Chapter Seventeen
Birds and Writing

When Flora, our youngest daughter, went off happily to join her sisters at Woodville School I looked around for something to fill my days. I decided on writing and bird watching.

Charlie gave me a typewriter. I took a correspondence course in writing with the London School of Journalism and a source of great happiness opened up. Over the years I had pieces published in British newspapers and magazines but I wrote mainly for The Buenos Aires Herald, the English language daily whose editor Robert Cox, and after him, when threats to his life and that of his family forced him leave the country at the time of the Military Dictatorship, James Neilsen, who both took a most encouraging interest in my stories about life on a Patagonian sheep farm.

Birds I had always enjoyed. Now I took Charlie's field glasses and started to observe them carefully. I soon found that some sort of guide was necessary. One afternoon Charlie brought two men up to the house for a cup of tea. They were oddly dressed and seemed a little uncomfortable; I took them for teachers on some sort of camping expedition but I was mistaken. The smaller and more talkative was a member of a well known family from Bariloche and owned a zoo in Germany. The bigger and quieter was Canadian, an expert on birds; they were on an expedition to do with studying the migratory habits of a certain sort of goose.

When the talk turned to birds I mentioned that I was trying to learn about them and needed some sort of guide. The Canadian immediately noted down an odd looking address, Sr Claes Olrog, Universidad de Tucuman, Tucuman, and suggested that I write there. I thought about it for some weeks and then did so, without any idea that I was writing to top name in Argentine ornithology at that time.

Several months later the answer came in almost illegible handwriting. Mr Olrog asked me to forgive his delay in answering my letter, he had been 'en el campo'. He had no copy of his guide which was out of print, and suggested that I write to Sr Rumboll, Museo de Ciencias, in the city of La Plata. So I did. I had quite forgotten this leisurely correspondence when, the following summer, the owner of the second address dropped in on his way back from a working trip to the south of Patagonia to give me his own copy of Claes Che Olrog's guide to Argentine birds, the only one then available. Now there are various as the Asociación Ornitológica del Plata expands with the increase of interest in the subject.

Every afternoon from March until June when it grew too cold and most of the birds had gone, and then again from September until our daughters came home from school at the beginning of December, I walked the fields round Leleque homestead with field glasses noting down all I saw in the way of birds.

Flora started at Woodville in 1968; Charlie became General Manager in 1970. From then on we drove at least twice a month to San José, Pilcaneu, Alicura or La Adolfina in the Province of Buenos Aires. I accompanied him with my binoculars and so, in the last years, did Truco.

Though we referred to him as a parrot Truco was really a parakeet (enicognathus ferruginius), according to Narosky and Yzurieta's guide to the birds of Argentina and Uruguay. In winter flocks of these shining green birds with elegant tails of chestnut red came down from the mountains to feed on the red berries of the hawthorn trees. One of our daughters found him at the foot of a poplar when he was no bigger than a mouse. We reared him on sunflower seed pre-chewed by one of us.

When he grew up the green of his feathers had a yellow tinge, he was smaller and shabbier than his wild brothers and sisters. But looks have nothing to do with charm and Truco had plenty of that useful quality even as a featherless nestling patched with grey down stuck through with feather sprouts. He extended his neck like a periscope to peer around objects with a pair of knowing brown eyes, putting his round head, mostly beak, on one side as parrots do. As he waddled about, pin toed and full of self importance, he tripped over his own feet. He never dirtied in the house at night. Charlie, the earliest riser, would find him on the edge of his box and rush him out of doors.

We had supposed that when Truco was full grown he would join up with the wild parrots and fly back with them to the Cordillera in spring. He seemed both interested and alarmed when a flock settld in his pear tree, but whether instinct would have driven out fear we will never know because Truco did not learn to fly. We found out later that one of his wings was damaged —when he fell out of the nest perhaps- and never recovered.

A flightless bird is the most defenceless of creatures. Truco could not be left alone for long. Though he would much rather have stayed at home his family dared not leave him and he accompanied us everywhere, enchanting children, softening policemen's hearts, attracting attention and comment where ever he went.

"Does he talk?" was the first question strangers asked. The answer was no. He did not imitate human speech but he used a variety of sounds to make his meaning clear. In an affectionate mood he nibbled at the cheek beside him as he stood on the shoulder, drawing each hair of the eyebrow through his beak with loving murmurs that changed on the instant to a furious crrrr if someone touched his tail. Fingers that approached his food when he was eating made him swear too, or a neck that moved when he was leaning against it taking a nap. A plaintive note repeated at intervals meant that something was wrong. When he was happy he sat in the little pear tree at the back of the house whistling and shrieking, imitating other birds and repeating in an affectionate tone variations on his own name, truqui, truqui-tru, truqui-tru, truco.

A tunnel like wrinkle in a rug, a woodpile full of openings or a nest set him cooing happily. He had such a passion for nests that we wondered if he was a she. The thrush with whom he shared the honeysuckle outside the front door when we were reading on the grass beneath was upset when he wanted to share her nest. His appetite for sunflower seed, the staple of his diet, varied. He preferred to wander round the table at meal times picking here and there. The arrival of the tea tray was a daily excitement. He could eat chocolate icing faster than most people can eat a slice of cake and would stick his head into the milk jug to wash it down, coming up with a blob of milk on his beak.

The sight of water running from the garden tap brought Truco at his fastest. He would sit for a moment uttering a little hiccough only heard as a prelude to bathing, take a beakful of water, another, hold up a claw as if to test the temperature and then get right under the water, putting his head down and his tail up to let it run down his body. He flapped his wings, almost standing on his head; sometimes he lost his balance and rolled right over. When done he hurried to the handle of a basket, or a knee conveniently crooked, and climbed up using beak and claw to dry off, bedraggled and content.

Truco had been with us almost a year when one Christmas Eve he disappeared. We gathered under the big hawthorn tree to which he had been changed when the pear tree showed signs of wear, looking and calling long after his usual bedtime. There was no answering call, no small, green parrot climbed laboriously down until, reaching the nearest hand he was carried indoors, fed and put into his box for the night.

We thought of the sparrow hawk that had twice dived on him when he incautiously sunned himself at the very top of the tree, of the cats that would make a mouthful of him if they found him on the ground when no one was about, and went sadly indoors to change for a Christmas Eve party. Torches played over the tree when we got back home shone only on flickering leaves and branches. We went to bed feeling that to wish each other a happy Christmas next morning would be unbearable.

We were woken on Christmas morning by an incredulous shout from Charlie who thought he was seeing a ghost when he found Truco sitting hopefully on the edge of his box waiting to be taken outside. He must have climbed down the hawthorn and gone to visit his friend Floriano, the gardener, who was away spending Christmas with his family. Isabel, the cook, enjoying a late evening snack of gooseberries, heard him in the long grass behind the bushes, brought him in, fed him and put him in his box. That was a really happy Christmas!

But a flightless bird lives on borrowed time. When Charlie retired and we went to live in Esquel we tried to get Truco accustomed to a cage –but he couldn't bear it and nor could we. We made a high perch and tried to barricade the uprights in such a way as to make it impossible for him to get to the ground, but he seemed to be able to climb

past anything using his beak and claws. One day a strange cat surprised him on the ground. Joan found them before it could harm him,
but the shock was too much for Truco. He sat on Charlie's wrist all
evening without moving and when we looked into his box next morning he was dead.

Chapter Eighteen

On the Road

Once Charlie became General Manager we spent a lot of time driving roads, mostly dirt, mostly lonely. The loneliest of all, northwards to Pilcaneu or Alicura or north east by Jaccobacci to San José on the River Limay in central Patagonia, became very familiar.

We had our quota of nights by flooded rivers, dangerous skids, snowed up roads, break-downs and strange meetings but nothing as frightening as a journey we made while we still lived in Maiten. We were coming home after spending Charlie's yearly holiday at Chirú. Charlie had arranged with the book-keeper in Maiten that a day or two before we were due to start on the return journey he should send a telegram giving the condition of the roads in the pre-Cordillera. I don't know why he bothered. The telegram arrived, 'Caminos intransitables' and off we set as planned.

On the last day of the three day drive we left the Rio Negro valley in the morning. When we started to cross the high country south of the river the sky ahead was blue black, the colour that means snow. We slid and ploughed across a white landscape and reached the town of Jaccobacci at about four o'clock in the afternoon. While we had a hot drink in the hotel Charlie asked a man, reccomended as working in the provincial road department (Vialidad Provincial), about the state of the road to Ñorquinco. He said that it was clear of snow, as it was as far as Rio Chico, half way between Jaccobacci and Ñorquico.

It was dark by the time we crossed the bridge over the Rio Chico. Pools of water lay across the road and there were no car tracks in the snow on either side. We ploughed past several before the snow covered mud at the side of a pool gave way and the car came to a stop. Charlie was starting to dig out one of the front wheels when a dog barked. Where there is a dog there are people; he disappeared into the darkness to investigate. The children were fast asleep and the girl we had taken with us to help with them took the opportunity to tell me a story she had read in a newspaper about a family that had frozen to death when their car was stranded in the snow.

After a time Charlie re-appeared with a man on horseback who pulled us out and we continued on our way. As the road climbed up from the river the pools disappeared and it started to snow. The bushes were covered and I could no longer distinguish the line of the road when, an hour or two later, the lights of Ñorquinco appeared beneath us and we started to descend. There was no snow in Maiten valley and the iced up underparts of the car bumped and banged as we drove along the frozen road towards the warm haven of home.

To get to estancia San José we had to cross three hundred kilometres of rough, treeless uplands with palisades of rock around the hill-sides. It was a hundred and fifty kilometres from Jaccobacci to Aguada Guzman, four or five houses on a hill top; not long after we turned off the main road onto a track that led, ruler straight, between bushes to the edge of the valley of the River Limay near the homestead of San José.

The estancia was isolated although a few kilometres away, on the other side of the Limay, was an important road, busy by Patagonian standards, that joined the populous valley of the Rio Negro with it's orchards and string of towns to San Carlos de Bariloche. By 1979 the road that I had travelled thirty years earlier with Uncle Frank and Auntie Agnes was in the process of being paved.

There was no bridge over the river near San José. To cross it was necessary to light a fire to attract the attention of the ferryman and wait until he had rowed across and back again, a process that might take an hour and a half –ferrymen never hurry- and left one carless on the far bank. There was no telephone in San José. By car from the homestead it was a four hour drive to the nearest bridge, the schools, shops and hospitals of the valley where the Limay and Neuquen rivers united to become the Rio Negro.

The climate in san José was pleasant; fruit and vegetables grew well and ripened earlier than on the other estancias. Sometimes we came back with sacks of pears or pumpkins for Leleque and Maiten. Once, coming back from San José with a load of pumpkins, Charlie had a series of punctures and handed out pumpkins to kindly people in the tiny village of Rio Chico who helped him –an engine driver kept a train waiting in the station while he vulcanized inner tubes

"What are you?" asked one grateful but puzzled recipient, "A pumpkin salesman?"

David and Isabel were living in San José when Charlie became General Manager and we started going there. Isabel, a trained teacher with a vocation, taught her own children and all the others on the estancia. In the 1970's a dam was made on the river Limay about a hundred kilometres down river from San José; before we retired the homestead and the greater part of the property were at the bottom of the lake created by the Chocon Dam. The Chocon was the first of a complex of dams that have flooded the valley of the river Limay that had in it so much of beauty and of history. The electricity produced goes, I understand, mostly to Buenos Aires. It seems a pity to flood valleys to make factories; cities already too big bigger still.

Just after descending the hill from Aguada Guzman —an aguada is a water hole- an odd little building stood near the road from which a loop ran off to pass in front of it. It was a shrine built to house the bones of the Marucho. The building was the size of a small room; it was plastered without but not within. The drooping fences that enclosed it on three sides fluttered with streamers and plastic flowers. In the interior, grimy with the smoke of candles that stood on an iron frame in the centre, were letters and school books, wedding veils, shoes, objects of all sorts left there for the Marucho to bless, or in gratitude for his favours. His bones lay in a little coffin at one end. The lid was not nailed; if you cared to lift it you saw them there.

This was the story as Isabel told it to me. The Marucho was a boy who accompanied drovers and their herds across those waterless stretches in the days when there were only a few tracks; sometime, I imagine, in the early years of this century. Torta frita in its simplest form is flour and water mixed, made into cakes and fried in deep fat. It is eaten mainly by those who cannot afford bread or who, like drovers, are out of reach of an oven. The Marucho took a torta frita and for this he was killed. The man who did it was probably drunk, the boy almost certainly half starved. Who knows what really happened.

The body was buried, I expect, beneath one of those rude crosses that stand by roads and fords in Patagonia commemorating a death. The place acquired a reputation for miraculous properties and one day a widow, wealthy as wealth is counted in those parts, promised that if her daughter recovered from a gave illness she would house his bones. The girl recovered and the shrine was made.

Truck drivers grinding their way across that 'travesia' (desert crossing), from the bridge over the Rio Negro to Jaccobacci, made the shrine particularly their own. Huge trucks that dwarfed the little building drew up in front of it; the driver climbed stiffly down and lit a candle to the hungry little drover's boy.

In time David and Isabel moved on to Alicura and their place was taken by Loraine and Gloria. As the dam grew and the waters started to rise the property was gradually cleared of everything useful; machinery, the wire in the fences, gates, doors, windows, galvanised iron sheeting from roofs and, of course, the stock. I remember one of our last visits to San José for an incident that might have affected us more than the drowning of the property which was, after all, pre-announced and prepared for.

Gloria was expecting their second child and the first, Charlie, a particularly active little boy, was about two years old. We had had a midday asado out of doors and were sitting over it when Gloria, missing Charlie, went to look for him. He was nowhere to be found. Soon we were all searching, the deep, still pool at one side of the house in our minds. It was over half an hour later that I went to get a handkerchief and found him in our bathroom running the taps. By then the anxiety had brought on contractions in Gloria; her baby was not due for a month or two, nor was she physically strong. Loraine took a man to the river where they lit a fire to call the ferry. This man was to stop a car on the road to take him into Picun Leufu, the nearest town, go to the hospital and bring the doctor.

It was an anxious wait of five or six hours before he re-crossed with the doctor, a woman. She was annoyed, protesting that she was far too busy to leave the hospital but Loraine's messenger had refused to leave her side until she agreed to go with him. She gave Gloria an injection to calm the contractions and hurried back to

Picun Leufu.. A few days later Gloria left San José to wait for her baby in a more accessible place.

One day we left Alicura at four in the morning heading for La Adolfina, a day's run away in the province of Buenos Aires. It was still dark when we passed through Piedra del Aguila about an hour later and climbed the hill beyond from which, in daylight, there is a view of the Limay valley which widens out as the mountains are left behind. The paved road that now runs straight across the flat to Picun Leufu, was under construction. At the foot of the hill traffic was diverted onto the old road that ran near the river, under the hills that close the valley to the south.

From the top of the hill after Piedra del Aguila I noticed a number of lights on what I took to be the course of the road we were to follow and remarked to Charlie on the number of people travelling at that early hour. When we turned into the old road I expected to meet the vehicles but, though we saw a light or two ahead we met nothing. At last a light appeared close ahead. As we came up to it it disappeared; when I looked back it was there again.

"Probably a 'luz mala'", said Charlie when I exclaimed.

I had read that a 'luz mala' is phosphoresence from bones in decay and had imagined a faint, ghostly light but these were bright enough to be mistaken for car lights. We saw others, though not so close, and met one old truck.

The eastern sky was beginning to pale when we came to the end of the detour and drove onto the main road again. Looking back along the road under construction I saw a number of lights. So hard is it at times to believe the evidence of one's eyes that I heard myself remarking on how early the road workers began their day.

No one in those days passed a car stopped at the roadside without at least slowing down to find out if the occupants were in some sort of trouble. I remember sitting for hours one cold day on the road between Mamal Choique and Jaccobacci while Charlie and the owner of a car that had broken down struggled with some recalcitrant part of the engine. As time passed other cars drew up and after a while there were four or five men peering under the bonnet. We women stayed in our cars. Another time the favour was the other way. I sat on the verge of a dusty road with our small daughters, delighted with the break in a long day's driving playing in the dust and feeding a bird that hopped out of the bushes, while Charlie and a passer-by wrestled with some mechanical trouble. He ended up pulling us to the nearest service station.

Once we were stopped by a man who had broken down with a coffin with his son's body in it in the back of his truck. He asked us to turn back with him and the coffin. Charlie had pedigree rams on board that had to be in the Show grounds at a certain time. We were still far from our destination; we could not afford the hours it would take so instead we informed the police at the next town. I still see him standing there looking after us.

Another strange encounter took place nearer home. It was either late spring or early autumn and there had been heavy rains. We were going from Leleque to Pilcaneu and had left Ñorquinco some way behind when we came in sight of the untidy farm belonging to a family of Lebanese extraction, beside the river Chinqueniyen.

Charlie was driving unusually fast because he had been held up by some annoying detail at the last minute and his plans for that day in Pilcaneu and the next in Alicura were threatened. We came down the side of the valley, rattled across the bridge, passed the farm buildings and came to an abrupt stop 300 metres farther on. A stream had cut a channel one and a half metres deep by two wide right across the road exposing the culvert that now easily contained its docile waters.

Between the culvert and the fence stood a white pick up, its front wheels in the stream the back embedded in a muddy bank. The name of the province was written in black letters across the door. There is something about a government employee driving a vehicle paid for with the tax payer's money that is intensely irritating to the average farmer, and this one was not in the best of tempers.

As Charlie stepped grimly out of the Ford Falcon saloon the driver of the pick up scrambled up the side of the embankment and limped towards him, one foot twisted outwards. A rakish cap shaded a pair of diffident brown eyes; the cold wind blowing from the mountains blew apart the skirts of his coat to show, under a brave red lining, jeans that flapped against the wasted muscles of his thighs. Charlie's expression did not change, he merely transferred his gaze and his grimness to the pick up.

There was no help to be had at the farm. A woman, shouting to make herself heard above barking dogs, told us that her husband had gone to Ñorquinco in the tractor and the 'patron' was away. It was a case of do it yourself. Putting on a pair of rubber boots the crippled driver hopped about in the icy water digging mud from under the wheels while we collected stones to fill in the ruts. Neither at the first pull nor at the second, when the pick up had been jacked up and the wheels cleared more thoroughly, nor when we drove through the stream and tried from in front, was the Ford Falcon able to move the pick up more than a few inches.

We had been there for over two hours and Charlie was addressing the government official by the courtesy title of 'ingeniero', when two labourers strolled down from the farm. They were sent back to bring boards. The pick up was jacked up yet again and while two men levered a post under the back axle boards were worked in under the wheels. The last and most awkward was almost in position

131

when a jeep, the first vehicle to pass that way since we hurried down the opposite side of the valley, crashed through the stream and came to a halt dripping water onto someone's neatly folded windjammer. Several men jumped out; the owners of the farm.

"Get those boards out of the way and we'll have you out in a jiffy with the truck". And so they did.

Chapter Nineteen

The Hard Way

Had Woodville School accepted secondary school pupils as boarders, or had Charlie gone to live in the Big House at Pilcaneu when he became General Manager, as had been the custom, our daughters would have remained at school in Bariloche. Neither of these things happened. Woodville only accepted boarders of primary school age; the Board wanted Charlie in Leleque keeping an eye on the biggest and most profitable of the properties and on the sheep stud.

When our daughters finished their primary education they went to my old school, St Hilda's College, in a suburb of Buenos Aires. On our journeys back and forth we used the bus. Charlie drove us to Bariloche; from there, all going well, it was a twenty four hour journey to the terminal in Buenos Aires. One journey back after leaving the children in school remains very clear in memory.

I can think of nothing more depressing than a bus station and the people it shelters in the early hours of the morning, but there is something pleasantly relaxed about setting out on a long journey by bus. The rumble and scurry of Constitución station set one counting suitcases and revising tickets, unintelligible announcements over the public speaking system keep the nerves on edge in Aeroparque, but from the terminal, which was then in Plaza Once, buses rolled out to Rio Cuarto, Tucuman and other distant parts of the republic as unconcernedly as if they were going to Temperley or Olivos.

As our destination was Bariloche we carried a number of honeymoon couples; a group that had assembled to see off a pair was all that disturbed the businesslike calm of the bus station. As we settled into our seats a youth in an Edwardian style jacket stepped up to their window and wrote beneath it. This addition to the respectable facade of our bus was much appreciated by his companions and amused lorry drivers and dawdlers in doorways as we lumbered out of the city.

Once out on the plains, free of traffic, we showed our speed and were washed by showers of rain that fell here and there from black cloud centres, making muddy roads muddier still, soaking brown stalks of rotting sunflower and spreading still wider sheets of water in which fences drowned and trees were islanded.

Some hours passed; it was about five o'clock in the afternoon when we made an unscheduled stop at a lonely service station by which stood another bus surrounded by its passengers. The door of our coach opened, some conversation passed and then the stewardess showed a young woman into the empty seat beside me. She was attractive, blonde, flushed and slightly dishevelled. We exchanged good afternoons.

"I made it!" she exclaimed delightedly.

She had been travelling on a bus that after limping along for some time had finally broken down and stopped by the service station we had just passed. Seeing a long distance bus approaching she had run to the roadside and stopped it; our driver had good naturedly taken her aboard, and here she was on her way while the rest of the passengers waited for a replacement bus that would probably be hours in arriving.

"And I must get to Santa Rosa," she said.

I asked her where she had come from.

"My home town, Los Toldos. I dont expect you have heard of it."

But I had. I studied her more attentively. Brown eyes and a darkish skin gave the lie to fair hair drawn tightly back from her face; decision showed in her expression as much as in her reaction to the breakdown, a latent dynamism too perhaps. She was not unlike another blonde who spent her early years in Los Toldos.

We read our magazines. When we stopped at Trenque Lauquen for something to eat she walked away from the rest of the passengers and ordered herself a coke and sandwiches. It was raher obviously deliberate, and when we were on our way again she explained that as she was not a legitimate passenger on the bus she was careful to pay for her food.

As it was growing dark by that time we talked more and read less. She was the eldest of the three daughters of a widow who lived in the town of Los Toldos. The other sisters had married young but my companion had gone on after finishing her secondary education to study geography in the nearby town of, I think, Lincoln. Now she had qualified and intended to do a course in geology in the University of La Plata.

"Thats a long way off," I commented. "Your mother will miss you."

"My boy friend doesn't like the idea either," she said. "I am on my way to meet him now in Santa Rosa."

As the hours passed this young man loomed larger and larger in our conversation. She had sent him a telegram saying that she would arrive on a certain day without specifying the hour.

"I'm afraid he will have been meeting buses all day long. This one was the last that makes the connection with Los Toldos. It should have arrived in Santa Rosa at eight o'clock. I wonder if he'll still be waiting? He'll be very angry." Then, firmly, "Well I'll be angry too." And a little later. "I made him an apple tart."

She was getting more and more agitated as the time went on and when half past eight came, then nine o'clock and still the lights of Santa Rosa remained hidden in the darkness, her nervousness communicated itself to me. Our hearts rose when at last the tops of the trees in the long avenue that leads to the city showed against the lower rim of the moon, but sank again when our driver turned into a service station a kilometre or two outside.

You will stop here for dinner," was her first anguished reaction. But it wasn't as bad as that; the driver had merely chosen this unfortunate moment to fill up with gas.

It was about half past nine when we stopped in front of a restaurant on a street corner opposite the bus station in Santa Rosa. She had her bags ready; the apple tart was in her hand; I handed her her coat, she gave me a kiss and when I last saw her was hurrying across the tarmac towards the terminus building. I turned into the restaurant with the rest of the passengers and sat down at a table feeling as though someone had snatched my book away in the most interesting part of the story.

Dozing and waking to drink cups of coffee or refuse them the rest of the night passed. Dawn as we left the valley of the Rio Negro, yet another cup of coffee in Piedra del Aguila, mountains growing higher and closer, the valley of the Limay and punctually, twenty four hours after leaving Plaza Once, the final stop in Bariloche.

The memorable part of that journey ended for me in Santa Rosa. I wish I knew if my blonde friend met her 'novio' and what he was like. I hope she has a longer life and a happier one than Eva Peron, that other blonde who spent her early years in Los Toldos.

The Company stopped helping to pay children's education when they were seventeen and had finished, or were about to finish their secondary schooling. We told our daughters that we could give them three years more of study and then they must start to earn their own livings. Moira chose to become a translator to start with, a three year course, Joan was only interested in veterinary science, a six year course at the University of Buenos Aires and Flora decided for journalism because she couldn't think what to do and the syllabus attracted her.

When they left St Hilda's College they lived in a flat in the centre of Buenos Aires. Moira was twenty one, Joan twenty and Flora seventeen when Isabel Peron's government was unseated. It was obvious beforehand that something was going to happen. After a visit we left the flat well stocked with tinned foods in case there was a period of disorder, but when the coup came it was quickly over.

Once in power the military proceeded to attack everything and everyone opposed to their rigid, right wing way of thinking. Things were bad in Argentina —but then they had been for years. I remember wondering some years after Peron had been exiled and the Peronist party, the majority, was still banned from standing in elections, how we would get back to representative democracy. The answer was, we now know, the hard way.

Films like The Official Story give only part of the picture. As usual in real life as opposed to fiction, the story of that stormy period of Argentine history is much less black and white —at least as it appeared to an Argentine citizen far from the centre of events. By 1976 army and civilians had suffered brutal attacks; elderly politicians, doctors attending the wounded, officers with their wives and families had been shot and blown up. Barracks had been attacked and aeroplanes hijacked.

The violence in the late sixties and early seventies even touched us in Patagonia. Cabinets of bullet proof glass with armed guards inside appeared in all banks. One of the guerillas' methods of getting money to buy arms was assaulting banks; another was kidnapping wealthy people or the heads of companies and holding them to ransom.

If anyone rang the front door bell in Leleque after dark during those years, not a common occurrence, I kept an eye on what was going on outside through the front windows. I even wondered about arranging some sort of code message with Ernesto, the book keeper, to pass to him over the phone that connected our house with the office, should anyone get the idea that it might be worth kidnapping the General Manager of The Argentine Southern Land Company.

When our car broke down in front of the barracks at the entrance to Esquel Charlie walked to the sentry box to ask if we could use their phone to speak to a garage stepping very slowly, his hands well away from his sides, like a character in a Western. One night when we had been to the cinema in Esquel and were returning after midnight we were stopped by soldiers who had a vehicle drawn up at the side of the road. When they had examined our car papers and identity cards we were allowed to carry on. As we passed the army truck I noticed a soldier lying on the ground beneath it with a machine gun on a tripod trained on us.

When General Aramburu was kidnapped Charlie had just become General Manager. We had driven to Estancia La Adolfina, a property in the province of Buenos Aires owned by the Company, and returned when the search organised by the police and the Armed Forces was at its height. We were stopped by police at a check point in the valley of the Rio Negro. Charlie went into a temporary shelter at the roadside to show the car papers and his personal documents. He came out and told me that mine had to be checked. I looked into my hand bag and found that I had left my identity card in Leleque, some six hundred kilometres away.

"You had better go and tell him," said Charlie. "I wont."

I went in and got the biggest dressing down of my adult life from that tired and harassed police officer. I do not remember being made to feel so small since I was called up before a particularly strongly spoken head mistress at St Hilda's College. He had to take the responsibility, which he did, for allowing us to continue on our way when I am sure he had the strictest instructions not to let anyone by without an identity card.

When the feeble government of Isabelita was removed and the Armed Forces took over most people breathed a sigh of relief and hoped for quieter times. We did not realise that bad elements were in control of the Armed Forces; violence had, as usual, bred violence; the usual dreary cycle of suppression, rebellion, repression. The military government struck out without discrimination at anything leftist or unconventional. Universities which had been a recruiting ground for guerillas, were especially controlled. Students were spied on, suspected, sometimes eliminated. Had I realised what was going on when Moira and Joan were attending the University of Buenos Aires I would not have slept during those years.

The head of the Buenos Aires police at the time had a flat in the same block as ours. His predecessor had been killed by a 'friend' his daughter brought home from the university they both attended. She left a bomb under the police chief's bed. An officer in civilian clothes came to the flat to ask our names, see our papers and, no doubt, inquire into our backgrounds.

When we made our annual visit to Buenos Aires in those years we always found the flat full of girls; friends from the University spending the night on the floor if there was no bed available, having a meal or a mate. Looking out of the window of our flat one day it struck me that the police chief's balcony was, perhaps, within bomb throw, certainly within gunshot. I remarked on it to one of our daughters and said,

"I hope you are careful who you invite here."

I did not find her answer, delivered with the cheerful confidence of youth, entirely reassuring.

"Our friends wouldn't do anything like that."

Mind you I think they had intelligence and common sense enough to have been on guard against anyone whose motives for friendship were entirely false.

Joan lost her student identity card, an essential in those days. She had to go from police station to police station to get a temporary one once passing, she told us, between a row of prisoners and police with guns trained on them. At last she heard through the mail that her new document was ready. I was in Buenos Aires at the time and accompanied her to the Central Police Station, where she was to collect it. We walked up the steps to the entrance and into a room at one side where a young policeman and an older one attended the public. A bomb had exploded in the dining room of the police station killing a number of people, the building that I remembered crowded with people coming and going and standing in queues stood silent, the steps empty.

The young man was smiling and chatty as he attended our pretty daughter. The older one had a poker face and a pair of dead, brown eyes. When Joan handed in her temporary document and was told to go into the building to get the new one I held out my identity card and made to go with her.

"Usted, señora, a la vereda," said the older man.

I sat in a café across the street watching the steps for an uneasy half hour until Joan came down them smiling and waving her new identity card. She had lost her way in the empty passages.

Things might have been so different. Had, say, one of our daughters fallen in love with a politically minded boy with leftist tendencies, got involved in a political group, or even if they had been unlucky enough to be in the wrong place at the wrong time. The son of friends who fell in love with a member of a left wing group while attending university was banished from the country, and lucky to get away with it. We heard of other young people who were imprisoned and were told that one or two children of a doctor in El Bolson known for his communist views, 'disappeared'.

The daughter of a professor of veterinary science who worked regularly in the Leleque stud was arrested with her husband. They were teachers at the University of La Plata. Both were set free after a few months, presumably innocent of whatever they had been accused of. She had a baby by the roadside while being transferred from one secret jail to another. She was put back into the car with the umbilical cord still attaching her to the baby. When they arrived at their destination a doctor came out to the car and cut the cord and she was taken to a room where she expelled the afterbirth. She was then made to remove her clothes and wash the stretcher, the floor and her dress.

Her father did not tell us this. We read her story in Nunca Mas. When the members of the Military Junta were tried this woman was one of the witnesses for the prosecution. Only after reading Nunca Mas did I realise to what depths of wickedness the Military Dictatorship of 1976 to '85 had sunk. I was one of many. The average citizen only understands the meaning of the events that make history years after they occur. Once we understood what had been going on, after the Malvinas War and Nunca Mas, then the Argentine people as a whole went out on the streets to back the constitutional government.

When I read criticisms by people who were not there of those who did not speak out against the Military Dictatorship at the time I think how easy it is with hindsight to make moral judgements. And how wrong.

Chapter Twenty
Esquel and Trevelin

Charlie retired from his job as General Manager at the end of 1979 and we went to live in Esquel. While he was running Maiten we had bought a fruit farm on the lower slopes of the Piltriquitron, the dramatic crag that looks over the town of El Bolson to hills covered in ciprés and mountains beyond. When we went to Leleque, which besides being a bigger job was farther from El Bolson, Charlie no longer had time to look after the place. I am no administrator so we sold it and bought a house in Esquel for the day we retired.

It is a high, square single story house just outside the centre of the town, built by a Welshman some seventy years ago when Esquel was a tiny village. After nearly thirty years of running big, sprawling houses all I asked was that our new home should be small –so that I did not have to rely on domestic help- and have a garden. It qualified on both counts and has, as well, a view from the back of a massive buttress of the Nahuelpan mountain, orange black in summer, white and grey in winter, that looks over Esquel from the south.

Moira said that the house reminded her of someone wearing a hat too small for them. The roof of corrugated iron sheeting hardly extends beyond thick walls of rosy coloured brick. At the front there is a high porch with a carved wooden decoration round the top. The doors and windows are high and rather narrow; they have band lights over them. There are two bedrooms, a sunny living room and, at the back, a kitchen, bathroom and pantry on either side of a black tiled passage. All the rooms have high ceilings and all except the bathroom and pantry, have wooden floors. A thick wall separates the front garden from the street; at the back there is a garden fifty metres long by fourteen wide. Looking towards the Nahuelpan when the trees are in leaf there are only a few chimneys to remind one that one is in a town.

Esquel lies in a hollow. Eastwards rises a bare, dark range and to the west, farther off, is the Cordillera, snow topped for the greater part of the year. Like the town of Trevelin some twenty kilometres into the mountains, Esquel was founded nearly a hundred years before we went to live there by the Welsh colonists who landed on the Patagonian coast near what is now the city of Puerto Madryn, in 1865.

When we came to live in Esquel it had 14.000 inhabitants, fifteen years on there were 25.000. Empty spaces were being filled in and the fields around the town being covered with housing estates and bungalows for renting out to tourists. The main industry was tourism. As Esquel is a centre for north western Chubut there are law courts, numbers of schools, several sanatoriums, a hospital, a jail and other government institutions.

Esquel is, or was before the paved road was finished, a good hour's run south and west of Leleque. We set out from our home of twenty years in the first days of January 1980 after an emotionally exhausting round of farewell parties; Isabel and Ester weeping as they watched us drive away. It was the end of a chapter for us all.

Truco sat, as usual, on the back of the front seat, disturbed by the presence of a cat in a box among the bags on the back seat. Moira was hitch-hiking in Europe; Joan and Flora travelled in the truck with their horses. Also on the back seat of the car was a brand new television set; a present from everyone on the estancia.

"You should see what **we** are going to give you," Ester had said to me a day or two before the official presentation, longing to spill the beans then and there. Television was something new in that part of the world.

That television set was a great comfort while we adjusted to our new surroundings. Retiring from a job long held can be compared to moving a well established bush from one part of the garden to another. Taken at the right time and moved to the right place the change can be beneficial but the actual move is traumatic. Settled habits of work and relaxation must be changed and while new ones form there are gaps. Television, we found, was an excellent filler of gaps.

A hundred kilometres in mountainous country, twenty for that matter, can make a great difference in climate. In Leleque it sprinkled rather than rained; in Esquel, 150 metres less in height above sea level, the rain fell in drops, not big ones but enough to make an umbrella and raincoat necessary. The air was milder and damper. The clustered houses with fire-places and heating spoiled the crystal of the air but held off frost. It was unusual in Leleque to have a second flowering of roses; in Esquel the second flowering in March and April was often the best. Plum, apple and, especially, cherry trees did well. In late summer we ate peaches from our garden.

It was strange to hear the Company spoken of as 'las estancias de los Ingleses' when we had been working with our Argentine owners for years. I learned not to try and set people right; an expression of disbelief crossed their faces.

Mrs Roberts, the wife of the butcher, asked our daughters to give her son, who was coming up for the final examinations in his secondary schooling, coaching in English. When the Malvinas Conflict broke out a year and a half later this lad was doing his military service. Thankfully his unit was not taken across to the islands though they got as far as waiting by the air field in Comodoro Rivadavia for transport.

On the coast of Argentina south of where the bulge of the province of Buenos Aires ends at Bahia Blanca and the continent slims right down, a triangular peninsular, the Valdés peninsular, juts out from the general south westerly line of the coast. There, fifty kilometres apart, lie the cities of Puerto Madryn and Trelew; due west across the continent are Esquel and Trevelin. All were founded by the Welsh colonists. Our neighbour in Esquel, whose father built he house we live in, is descended from the man for whom Trelew is named. Trelew is a Welsh name meaning the town of Lewis just as Trevelin means the town of the mill.

The first group of Welsh families to colonise this part of Patagonia, 153 men, women and children, sailed from Liverpool in May 1865 arriving off the Valdés peninsular a month later. The ship they sailed in was called the Mimosa, a name that brings the Mayflower to mind. These men and women, like the Pilgrim Fathers, were leaving the British Isles to build a new life. They were emigrating to escape the pollution, as they saw it, of their language and religion by the people who were crowding into Wales to work in the mines.

It is difficult to understand how anyone would choose to make a colony on that barren coast. They lived at first in caves on the beach and June is winter in Patagonia. A young man wandered off after they landed to have a look around and was never seen again. It was supposed that he got out of sight of the sea, lost his sense of direction and wandered about the waterless hills until he died of thirst. His skeleton was found years later.

That the Welsh colony survived was due to the help they received from the Argentine government that encouraged any effort to colonise Patagonia; that they remained and, eventually, prospered was due to their religion, the sense of community it gave them, and to their good relations with the indigenous peoples. Alcohol, which had such a destructive effect on the Indians and their relations with the settlers, was not available in the Welsh colony. Instead they exchanged bread for the meat they so often lacked.

While their elders struggled to tame cows for milking, grow wheat and tame the waters of the Chubut river at whose mouth they had settled, the younger generation learned from the Indians to ride and to hunt. From them they heard of a land to the west, a land of rivers, lakes, trees and mountains. It must have sounded like paradise to settlers struggling in that colourless, infertile country of stones, sand and bush.

In about 1890 a group of Welshmen set out from the coast with troops of sheep and cattle and settled in the wide and fertile basin in which the town of Trevelin now lies. They sowed wheat and made a mill to grind it, the mill for which the town is named. What is left of it is a museum. The Welsh community in Patagonia cherish their traditions, the stories of what their ancestors did and endured.

A school-house on the outskirts of Trevelin is kept as a memorial to another episode in the history of the Welsh colony. In the early years of this century Argentina and Chile agreed to ask the British crown to arbitrate in the question of the long frontier between the two countries. Edward Vllth named Thomas Holdich head of the commision that was to decide the line of the frontier. I think that it was then decided to use the watershed rather than the line of the highest summits as the de-limiting factor.

The watershed lies well to the east of Esquel but as the area was already settled Holdich called a meeting of the Welsh settlers to decide whether they wished to be Chilean or Argentine. They had always been Argentine and voted to remain so. The little school-house where this historic vote was taken is kept as it was then with photographs of the occasion and books of signatures.

Delicious 'Welsh' teas with home made butter and bread, jams, scones, tarts and cakes are served to appreciative tourists in Trevelin; tea is not part of Argentine culture either as a drink or a meal. There are pageants to commemorate anniversaries; boys dressed as Indians riding bareback holding spears made of coligue, a cane that grows in the mountains, the parson on horseback carrying a huge bible, the farmer bringing his family to chapel for Sunday service in a four wheeled vehicle drawn by two horses. There are shows of farm produce with prizes for the best fruit or vegetables, the finest home made butter, the best fruit cake, known here as Torta Galés.

I know little about the Welsh nation. Their descendants in Patagonia, considered as a community, seem to combine a hard headed, practical attitude to life with a deep respect for things of the spirit. Perhaps their history as settlers in a hostile environment accentuated these two strains in the national character; the practical without which they could not have survived, the spiritual that consoled them for the hardships they endured and gave them the strength to carry on.

Every year there is a mini-Eisteddfod in Trevelin. The one we attended was held in a school. The hall that held three or four hundred people was packed. The programme covered two and a half pages of foolscap in double spaced typing. It listed over forty competitions, in singing mostly, from solos to choirs of twenty to thirty voices; there were also recitations and a few handicraft competitions. One of the main groups of singers was from El Maiten, one from the coastal cities, a third was local.

A Master of Ceremonies and several assistants chatted their way through the programme. The announcing was in Spanish, the language of every day, and so were twenty of the competitions. Fifteen had names like Rwy'n gweddio drosoch chwi or Brawdegefo'r llythyren. The Baird's crown was open to anyone, whether they had Welsh blood or not, who could write a poem good enough to win it in either language. The achievement of the Welsh is not only to have retained their culture but to have shared it, enriching both themselves and Argentina.

The results of the competitions together with an analysis by one of the judges of the reasons for their decision, were interspersed among the other items. Prizes were handed out on the spot. This being a mini-Eisteddfod (a full blown Eisteddfod is held every year in the coastal communities) it started at half past two in the afternoon. As the hours passed the air in the hall grew stuffy. As it grew colder outside the white slopes visible through the windows were blurred by moisture collecting on the glass before being swallowed up in the early darkness of a winter afternoon. Still the competitors followed each other onto the stage and broke into song or verse as if it were the most natural thing in the world, and still the audience listened attentively and clapped politely or with enthusiasm.

Shortly after the interval the master of ceremonies warned us that the most significant moment of the Eisteddfod was approaching, the crowning of the Bard, the winner of the competition for the best poem presented. 'As a man's spirit,' he said, 'was his highest attribute and poems were the highest expression of that spirit, poets were deserving of the highest honours.' I wonder how the average member of the average rural community would re-act to that statement.

When the time came for the Bard to be crowned a carved wooden throne was dragged centre stage. Lights were trained on it, a soloist and two children with bouquets of flowers took up positions near it. The poems entered had been sent away to be judged. The winner was asked to stand when the envelope containing the judge's decision and his reasons for arriving at it, was opened and the result read out; the children would bring him or her to the throne. Even we who did not understand all that was going on, could feel the tension building up in the hall.

On this occasion there was anti-climax. The Master of Ceremonies read out the judge's letter in a voice heavy with disappointment. He had not considered any of the poems presented good enough to earn the writer a Bard's crown.

Chapter Twenty-One
The Malacara

Going to Trevelin from Esquel just before one reaches the town, a road leads off to the right. On a sign post with an arrow pointing along it is written, La Tumba de la Malacara. A malacara is a horse with a white face, an extra wide white blaze. This one earned a place in the history of European settlement in Patagonia as a gallant protagonist in one of the few violent episodes in the relationship of the Welsh settlers with the indigenous peoples.

The Malacara belonged to a Welsh settler on the Atlantic coast from whom he was stolen by Indians from the Cordillera in 1877. In 1883 the leaders of the colony decided to investigate the truth of the stories the Indians told of a wonderful country to the west. Four men were chosen to go on this mission. One or two of them were well on in years; the youngest, John Evans, was only twenty one. Landing from the Mimosa as a baby he belonged to the first generation of settlers to grow up in Patagonia. He had learned from the Indians how to survive in that desolate environment, was strong, adventurous, an excellent rider and knew the country well.

The four men set out on horseback at the end of the year, travelling with a troop of horses that were let loose to graze at night. One morning when they were rounded up, instead of the nineteen that had been set loose the night before there were twenty. They had been joined by a malacara. Studying the horse they came to the conclusion that it was the one that had been stolen six years earlier. He was strong, tame and willing and was given to John Evans to use.

Early on in their journey they came in contact with a tribe of Araucanos whose head was the cacique Foyel. In the wake of the Desert Campaign they were being hunted out of their strongholds in the Cordillera. It was not a good moment for peaceable, lightly armed men whose religion forbade the taking of human life, to be investigating the area.

In March, three months after that first contact with the Araucanos, the Welsh party was camped in the vicinity of what is today the town of Gualjaina in the valley of the river Chubut some ninety kilometres east of Esquel. Two Indians, one of whom they recognised from the first meeting, appeared and insisted that they come with them to see Foyel. Evans and one of his companions went with them but when, after a certain distance there was still no sign of a tolder’a, they turned back in spite of the Araucanos who alternately persuading and threatening tried to make them carry on.

Discussing the matter the Welshmen decided that the Indians were planning some mischief and that their best course was to get back to the coast as quickly as possible. They set off at once. When they reached the river Chubut, at its lowest by the end of the summer, they walked their horses in the water for forty kilometres and left it at a gravelly place where hooves made no imprint. In this way, concealing their tracks as best they could, they rode for three days and nights. By then the older men were so exhausted that they had to be tied to their saddles and driven along in the troop.

They were following the valley of the Chubut and decided to stop and rest at a place, some distance from the river, where there was a spring surrounded by rocks that could be used as a defence. Reaching the place at midnight they found that the spring was dry. Two of the horses were too tired to carry on that night so Evans remained with them while the rest of the party rode to the river and camped beside it. In the morning he picked up their tracks and followed them to the camp where they remained all that day and the following night.

The next morning, a Sunday, they set off again. Evans saddled his best horse, the Malacara, and went off with his dogs to hunt for fresh meat, catching up with the others at midday with two Patagonian hares tied to his saddle. He transferred them, together with an old Remington, to one of the pack horses and had a good meal of charqui, dried guanaco meat. They were by now well on towards the coast and beginning to feel safe.

At about three o'clock in the afternoon when they were moving steadily along the north bank of the river the Malacara began to show signs of nervousness, tossing his head and pulling at the reins. Then they heard yells and drumming hooves. Shielding their bodies behind their horses, the blades of their spears glinting, thirty to forty Araucanos galloped down on the little party of Welshmen and, parting to right and to left, made a circle round them. Evans had a glimpse of one of his companions on the ground with two spears in his body, of another swinging his machete, as he rode the Malacara at a space between two Indians. He deflected a thrown spear with his arm as they broke through the circle. In four bounds the Malacara had gained twenty metres when they found themselves on the edge of a cutting four metres deep made by water running to the river.

Evans gave the Malacara a crack on either side with the maneas, a strap for hobbling horse that he carried in his hand, and put him at the cliff. The horse responded with a leap that carried him far out and landed with his quarters under him, fore legs extended. With a wild heave he gathered himself to his feet and galloped on. The Araucanos, expecting to find man and horse with broken limbs at the foot of the cliff, took an easier way down. That space of time was enough to put Evans and the Malacara out of reach of boleadores.

A stretch of pampas grass offered concealment but Evans galloped on until he found a place where the river could be forded. The bank on the far side was too steep for the Malacara until Evans dismounted and helped him, pulling on the reins. Looking back as they made their way up the southern side of the Chubut valley Evans saw the pampas grass burning furiously. While the main body of Indians carried on on the farther side six had crossed the river in their tracks.

That night and the next day they made their way across barren, rocky country, Evans choosing the steepest, most difficult route to confuse the men who were tracking them. In the darkness they walked into a herd of sleeping guanaco; in the confusion of bolting animals Evans thought for a moment that they were Indians. Horse and man grew more and more thirsty as one after another the springs he looked for proved to be dry. When, at last, on the second night they found water the Malacara, after the intense physical effort followed by long thirst, got colic and they could only move on at intervals. The next morning they saw what Evans both longed for and dreaded, a man on horseback. He proved to be a Welshman hunting guanaco and was able lend Evans a horse.

It was over a week before a party from the colony, armed by Colonel Fontana, the Governor of the territory, and guided by Evans, arrived at the place of the Indian attack. When he saw the clouds of chimangos and caranchos wheeling above it Evans could bring himself to go no nearer.

What was left of the bodies, hacked by Indians, torn by animals and birds of prey, was buried. One can picture the little group of roughly dressed men standing round the grave in that immense, desolate landscape, singing the Welsh hymns that make even death less dreadful. The place has been known ever since as the Valley of the Martyrs.

Evans never forgot what he owed to the Malacara. He offered to buy him off the original owner but all that he could afford was not enough. A good horse was worth more than money. The quarrel between the two men was only settled when the colonists, being gathered together to discuss some question to do with the irrigation system, the question was put to them. Whom should the horse belong to, the man from whom it was stolen or the man who had found it and whose life it had saved? All hands but one were raised in favour of John Evans.

Evans' interest in the Cordillera survived his experience in the Valley of the Martyrs. He helped organise and was one of the group of the men from the colony on the coast who set out in 1888 to settle the fertile basin whose centre today is Trevelin. He became a leading citizen of the town running the flour mill and, later, the telephone exchange. Secure in his master's affection, following him to the mill each day the Malacara passed his old age.

When he died Evans buried him in a grassy place by the canal that carried water to the mill. A rock pushes up beside the wooden railings that enclose the grave. On it in neat capital letters, unevenly spaced where irregularities in the surface have made the engraver's job difficult, is written;

AQUÍ YACEN LOS / RESTOS DE MI CABALLO / EL MALACARA QUE ME / SALVO LA VIDA EN EL ATA- / QUE DE LOS INDIOS EN EL VA- / LLE DE LOS MARTIRES EL 4- / -3-84 AL REGRESARME / DE LA CORDILLERA.

RIP
JOHN D.EVANS

Chapter Twenty-Two

A Bitter Experience

I was seventeen when I left school at the end of June 1939. A few months later England declared war on Germany. We gathered in the drawing room at Chirú on a Sunday to hear King George VIth speak to his people. The frail, halting voice issued from a dome shaped wireless set that stood on the music stand that my grandmother had carved in long, slow days in the little house at the centre of a circle of plain.

The King ended his message with a quotation from St Thomas á Kempis that has accompanied me through life. 'Go out into the darkness and put your hand into the hand of God. That will be better than any light and safer than any known way.' The silence in the room when he finished speaking was broken by the sound of the bell rung in the dining room to let us know that lunch was on the table. As we walked along the hall my father blew his nose. That familiar trumpet sound signalled the end of one life and the beginning of another.

Of the four young adults gathered in the drawing room at Chirú that Sunday (a cousin, Jim, had ridden over to join us) Tony, my brother, and Jim were dead, my elder sister and I widows by the time the Second World War ended. Jim was the first to go when the plane he was piloting was shot down over the Channel; Tony's plane crashed into the Burmese jungle. My sister's husband went down with his ship in the Mediterranean, mine was killed in a training flight over the

Midlands in 1943. Both were Argentine volunteers. I have heard that no British community outside the Commonwealth provided more volunteers to the British Armed Forces during the Second World War than the British community in Argentina.

I decided to be a nurse; not through any sense of vocation, I was rather dreamy and impractical, but because it seemed to be a good thing to be in time of war. In March 1940 I began training in the British Hospital in Buenos Aires. Not the happiest period of my life but certainly useful. Before I finished the three year training I married Allan Cameron, Argentine born, Scottish educated, the son of New Zealanders. Allan joined the Royal Canadian Airforce in early 1942 and sent me a cable six months later asking me to go to Canada and marry him. We were married in Toronto in September of that year.

When Allan finished his training he and his companions were taken across the Atlantic in one of the Queens, trans-Atlantic liners made before the war and adapted as troopships. The great ships packed with fighting men did the trip in three days. I went to New York to volunteer, for some reason I could not do so from Canada. The ship I travelled on with its heterogeneous collection of passengers; military and civilian, American, British, Australian, wives, officers, soldiers, even a child or two, was one of a convoy. The journey took three weeks from the day we embarked in New York to the day we left the ship in Bristol, England. We saw no land in that time, just grey seas, grey sky and a grey tanker rolling among the waves beside us. We had to carry our life jackets with us always and were given points to make for if the signal for an emergency was sounded, but there was no boat drill as there is on passenger ships in peace time. Perhaps it wasn't worth it on a packed ship in those cold seas near Iceland.

What a joy it was to see gulls, then the coasts of Ireland and Scotland. No one could bear to go down to their cabins that evening. An officer leaning on the deck railing sang 'The Mountains of Mourne' as we passed them in long summer twilight. We volunteers were collected by authoritative women at the station when we arrived in London and taken to a hotel.. The sheets on the beds were blood red; more startling in those days when sheets were always white, than it would be today.

I nursed in Pembury County Hospital, south of London. German planes flew overhead on their way to bomb London. When the air raid warning sounded and we heard the distinctive beat of the German aeroplane engines old ladies, many of them evacuees from London, would tremble in their beds. On an outside verandah a row of beds was occupied by tubercular patients. These chatty young women wanted to hear all about the country I came from. I am no singer. When they asked for songs I did my best with the Argentine National Anthem. They were as astonished to find that the words were in Spanish as they were at the fact that Argentina had a national anthem. Tobacco flowers scented the air at night reminding me of Chirú.

That strange wartime existence, meeting and parting, joy and pain, ended when Allan's plane crashed on a training flight on December 16th 1943. I worked for a few months in Guy's Hospital of which Emily Mcmanus who had been going to marry my uncle, Anthony Traill, who died of trench fever in the First World War, was Head Matron.

In January or February of the following year my brother Tony was killed. It seemed time that one of us went home to our parents. As my sister would not make the passage across the Atlantic with her little son until the seas were completely safe I left England when the flying bombs were falling.

The other war that has affected me closely was a very minor affair. As a name for the islands that caused it I prefer Falklands, there is a rugged sound to it, Malvinas is gentle. The double name is awkward and ridiculous, though no more so that the situation it describes. If only it was just a question of names!

To Argentines of British descent it is a particularly sensitive question. We belong to two countries: a little one with a long history whose people think well of themselves as its citizens and a big one with a short history whose people are inclined to under-estimate their country. As a result of their multi-racial heritage Argentines look outwards. The British people, when they look outwards, look towards the countries with which their history has connected them. The average citizen of the British Isles is not interested in South America.

It is not easy for people brought up to think of themselves as British to decide that they belong in Argentina. The reasons are historical as much as racial. Both England and Spain had intrepid explorers and huge empires. At one time they burned each others' subjects for religious reasons. England was a bumptious up and coming country when Spain was already a great power. Drake, depicted in my first history book rolling a last bowl before going off to defeat the Armada, is referred to in Spanish histories, with some reason, as a pirate.

The twice that Great Britain has used force to intervene in Argentine affairs it has had an effect out of proportion to the actual conflict. The first time, or times, as every Argentine school child knows, were the 'Invasiones Ingleses.' In the early nineteenth century Great Britain was still adding to her empire, picking up islands and countries across the globe. Spain was in a bad way during the Napoleonic Wars and South America looked temptingly undefended. In 1806 and then again in 1807 British fleets sailed across from South Africa and units of the British Army under Generals Whitlocke, Beresford and Popham Home made landings in the area of the estuary of the River Plate.

The Spanish Viceroy left for the interior of the country in a hurry and the 'criollos', the native born citizens of what would become Argentina, repelled the invaders without help from the mother country. The failed 'Invasiones Ingleses' were the impulse that set first Argentina, then Chile, Peru and Bolivia on the road to independence.

The Malvinas Falkland Islands had mattered to Argentines for at least a century before they sprang into the consciousness of the average Briton when the stupidity of General Galtieri turned a problem into a conflict. How many Britons could have placed the Falkland Islands on the map before 1982? For Argentines the problem began when Great Britain occupied them in 1833. I do not know the exact history, nor do I think it matters. What matters is that Great Britain found the Islands useful and strategically placed, decided that they were worth keeping and settled families on them. Being a much stronger and more influential country she could ignore Argentine protests and continued to do so.

We had been living in Esquel for just over two years when, on April 2nd 1982, Argentine troops landed on The Malvinas Islands. Some weeks later when we were in Trevelin on a Sunday watching karting races, the news spread through the crowd that British troops had landed on the Georgias. There was no longer any hope of avoiding a confrontation as there had been during the Task Force's long, leisurely passage from the north Atlantic to the south. That slow passage is somehow symbolic of the whole business; the waiting, the gamesmanship; General Galtieri gambling on Mrs Thatcher backing down, Mrs Thatcher expecting General Galtieri to run at the threat of force.

Even if either of them had had cold feet it was too late. The Argentine people had seen a dream come true; the British, after years of creditable but humiliating retreat from Empire, handing back countries their forebears had taken over, had found people who wanted them to stay.

The karting, the tiny cars running round and round the oddly shaped plaza in Trevelin with its big, dark pine trees could no longer hold our interest. We met a family of old friends and invited them home to tea. When we got there we turned on the television to entertain the children and saw The Merchant of Venice. It was the only time I saw a Shakespeare play, spoken in English, on our television.

Our friends had three children. One of them, a boy of eleven or twelve, was very quiet as we drove back to Esquel, his face both dreamy and bright. His great grandfather, head of the British railways in Argentina, had been knighted after they were sold. His son, the little boy's grandfather, came to live in northern Patagonia, joined the Royal Airforce at the start of the Second World War, proved to be an exceptional pilot, flew pathfinders, was shot down over Europe and escaped with the help of the Resistance, the stuff of a hundred movies. He flew a plane into old age. This boy had grown up hearing about aeroplanes and flying; he was dreaming now that he was old enough to pilot a plane against the British. He loved The Merchant of Venice.

A black out was ordered in Esquel. Charlie and I who knew about black outs, made an excellent job of our house tacking black paper over the band lights. Most people just went to bed early or dimmed down the inside lights. Some forgot altogether and left lights blazing in the darkish streets.

In Esquel, which is attracting more and more tourists, we were in contact with a lot of non-Argentines, mostly British or Australian, in the years following the Malvinas Conflict. Every one of them asked, sooner or later, what it had been like for people of British descent in Argentina at that time.

The Argentine people as a whole behaved with great consideration and kindness to those of us who lived among them. Shop assistants would change the conversation from the universal topic of the Malvinas when one went in. I only remember one hard look. It was from a man walking along the street when we went to the gate to see off some friends who worked for the United Nations, talking rather loudly in English. A small illuminated sign with a union jack, advertising a British insurance company was broken by a stone thrown at it...these were the only hostile reactions I noticed. In Argentina in general and Patagonia in particular, people matter more than nationalities.

Time Magazine has a Spanish language edition. I remember during that unhappy April and May seeing a middle aged, middle class Argentine woman bending over a copy of Time that showed on the cover a section of the riotous crowd that gathered to cheer British troops leaving for the Malvinas from, I think, Southampton. A girl had pulled off her shirt and was standing, naked from the waist upwards, waving it.

"How can they say goodbye to their men like that?" this Argentine lady asked with a puzzled expression. I did not try to explain that for many Britons a small, far off war is a kind of sport.

In my case the Malvinas Conflict was a bitter experience. It was bitter to feel ashamed of both my countries and their leaders; a tough, narrow woman and a very stupid general. It was bitter to feel ashamed of the country I was brought up to love and admire and of the country I live in and love.

I never felt any bitterness against the German people who caused so much sorrow and loss to my family —we seemed equally victims of history- but I had to fight a bitterness against Mrs Thatcher's England for years after this mosquito bite of a confrontation. Trying to understand myself I came to the conclusion that though for years my first loyalty had been to Argentina I kept in my mind a picture of a wise mother country inhabited by moderate, fair minded people. Perhaps my feelings were not so much bitterness as a re-action to the sentimental picture of England absorbed from my reading as a girl; Henty, Kipling, Galsworthy, Ian Hay, Bulldog Drummond, Saunders of the River, The Scarlet Pimpernel...I vow to thee my country...In Flanders Fields...We few, we happy few...

I was fortunate in that I subscribed to The Listener and so read some balanced, intelligent articles that showed not everyone in Britain believed they were engaged in a crusade. Unfortunately voices like The Listener's do not carry far. The tabloids with their blaring, shameful headlines were well quoted in Argentina.

Our youngest daughter, Flora, left for Australia on her first trip abroad on the day that Argentine troops, careful to shed no blood but their own, landed on the Islands. Beginning with a customs official at Sidney Airport she fought her country's battle with words. She was one against many; Australians heard only the British point of view. It came to the point, Flora told us, that her re-action to the news of a British vessel sunk was one of elation. She was horrified to find herself applauding an event that meant people had been killed and wounded.

How many of those people who cheered in the pubs when the poor, old battleship Belgrano was sunk by a nuclear submarine thought of the 323 men and boys who went down with her? From here it sounded as if the British people regarded Argentine lives as expendable, unimportant, a bit of a joke. They weren't people, just Argies or Wogs.

As people caught between two sides in an armed conflict have always known the targets of bombs and bullets on either side are ordinary men, clever, silly, vain or wise in the usual proportions. Courage and cowardice, brutality and gentleness are pretty evenly spread through the human race. The Argentine woman who dodged about the traffic on a busy street in Buenos Aires picking up oranges fallen from a bag my small daughter carried, the English woman who stopped one wet evening in Regent's Street to help me pick up packages fallen from an overloaded carrier bag, are the same woman.

When Mrs Thatcher did a victory dance outside 10 Downing Street after General Menendez surrendered and said, "Now England is great again." I felt very angry for the country my parents were so proud to belong to. How could the Prime Minister of Great Britain know so little of her country's history as to think that winning a small war with powerful backing against a much weaker country, added to its greatness?

The shame I felt for Argentina came later, after the humiliation of defeat and surrender, which was also a relief; I had always known we could not win. When I read Nunca Mas I understood for the first time that the fight against terrorism had deteriorated into an attempt to stamp out a way of thinking; that thousands of innocent people had suffered imprisonment, torture and death at the hands of the Military Dictatorship.

It was bitter to realise that in a sense we must be grateful for our defeat. Had Mrs Thatcher, like Winston Churchill, made a distinction between the government of the country she was fighting and its people, she could have claimed credit, as she tried to do ten years later, for bringing down the Military Dictatorship. But the only lives that mattered to her were the two hundred British ones she could lose and still retain the backing of the British people.

The Malvinas problem will only be solved when common interests and common sense take the place of childish nationalism.

Chapter Twenty-Three

Both Sides of the Andes

Once retired Charlie took jobs managing estancias and classing sheep. We made long drives for our own amusement; there had never been time while he worked in the Company. In February 1983 we drove south to have a look at the Moreno glacier on Lago Argentino, some 1100 kilometres from Esquel.

The glacier runs into Lago Argentino at a narrows where two branches of the lake unite. In its advance it closes off the passage between them. One of the branches has no other outlet for its waters and the pressure builds up until it bursts the barrier of ice. This happens every two or three years and tourists, scientists and photographers come from all over the world to see it. Though we did not know it this event was due when we went to see the Moreno glacier.

The Province of Chubut ends and Sta Cruz begins on the 46th parallel, some 450 kilometres south of Esquel, and stretches on south to the Straits of Magellan. We drove south on the Ruta Cuarenta, along the mountains and returned by the coast.

The country we drove through was desolate, a different sort of desolation as we got farther south, to the one we were accustomed to -greyer and darker. Even the lakes were different; great milky green stretches of water, sometimes more milk, sometimes more green, their eastern shores bare of trees. Our lakes farther north were blue or green, framed by mountains and set among trees.

Once a herd of about thirty guanacos stood on a slope above the road, their faces turned towards us, big ears spread, before bounding away on springs. When we crossed the upper reaches of the Rio Chico I remembered Musters and his Tehuelche friends crossing it when the water was floating with chunks of ice, early on in his journey from Punta Arenas to Carmen de Patagones. No wonder Leleque seemed like paradise to him.

The town of Calafate, an hour's drive from the glacier, was packed with people waiting for the ice barrier to give away. We were thankful to find a room, even though the door of the bathroom we shared with several others would not shut more than half way. We had difficulty in finding a place to sleep on all four nights of this drive; the towns we stayed in were either overfull or unprepared for travellers.

The Moreno glacier was worth a few bad nights. Nature has set the scene magnificently and, at least until 1983, the year of our visit, man had not been allowed to spoil it. There were no stands selling food or drinks, no cans or plastic bags. The glacier is in a National Park run by a government body responsible for areas of great natural beauty or interest that belong to the nation.

A space had been levelled on the hill-side opposite the glacier to make a car park. Paths crossed the slope beneath, flowers and bushes grew among them and there were rocks to sit on to contemplate the great river of ice that ended in a channel of rushing water at our feet, to count ice turrets or estimate tons of ice and the millions of years it had taken to form them.

"Parece un postre helado," said a woman. It was a good comparison, kilometres of pure white merengue formed into peaks and rifts by a cosmic cook with millions of years on his hands.

It was easy to sit gazing at the fantastic yet ordered world of ice turrets that stretched back between wooded mountain sides and up into cloud, at the cliff of ice over sixty metres high that ran back across the lake. Blue fissures seemed to widen by the minute; surely a great block of ice must break off and join the others melting into fantastic, greenish shapes as they floated on the water. Even comparatively small pieces of ice thundered as they fell. When a whole turret broke off, I read, it made as much noise as a three storey building collapsing.

Between the slope we sat on and the glacier, water rushed from a tunnel under the wall of ice that would eventually give way under the pressure building up behind it. This did not happen while we were there. When we arrived home on the afternoon of the fifth day to the largest town we had seen in that time, the modest bustle of Esquel seemed overwhelming.

We crossed over the mountains into Chile several times. It was a world away from the Argentine side of the Andes. Where the Atlantic coast of South America is near desert for the most part, the Pacific coast from a little north of Esquel southwards has one of the highest annual rainfalls in the world. In Chaiten, on the Pacific across the mountains from Esquel, the average annual rainfall is 8000 mm, in Esquel it is 600 mm, in Leleque 4 to 500 mm and farther east it goes down to 200 mm.

The mountains are an effective barrier between Argentina and Chile. Spanish as spoken in Chile and as spoken in Argentina can be compared to English as it is spoken in England and in the USA; the accent is different and different words are used for everyday things. In Chile nafta becomes bencina, an estancia is a funda and a colectivo a bus.

Another thing that strikes a Patagonian is the length of the history of European settlement in that country as far south as Puerto Montt and the Island of Chiloe, a little north of Esquel. The Spanish Conquistadores explored southwards from Peru down the Pacific coast of South America long before they made any impression on the Atlantic coast. The city of Osorno, across the mountains from Bariloche was celebrating the 433rd anniversary of its founding when we visited it for the first time in 1981. Esquel, of which no one we spoke to in that part of Chile had heard though they all knew of Bariloche, was 75 years old, Bariloche perhaps ten years older.

The first time we crossed into Chile we used a pass north of Bariloche, Paso Puyegue. On the Argentine side grey lakes reflected a grey sky; the thick woods on either side of the road were as gloomy as they were beautiful. From the Chilean border the road ran downhill and the sun came out to shine on a different world. Instead of tall, dense forests floored with coligue cane trees we did not recognise stood roped together by creepers. The coligue had been replaced by a richer, gracefully curving variety of cane that climbed into the trees, smothering some of the smaller ones. The road was bordered by wild fuschia bushes in flower. There was a growth, a lust for life in the vegetation that is usually associated with hot climates.

As we got lower tall, slender trees stood about small fields where black and white cattle stood knee deep in rich grasses that grew up to and enroached on the edges of the narrow, paved road. The quiet cow on signs that warn drivers in Argentina of the possibility of stock on the road ahead had been replaced by a prancing bull. That first afternoon was clear and we had a good view of a spectacular group of mountains; the perfect cone of Osorno, to one side a mountain topped by a pinnacle of rock, behind them the massive bulk of the Tronador. In the three days we were in Chile we never saw this magnificent trio free of cloud again.

Until 1977 there was no road running north and south along Chile south of Puerto Montt. One was made then by General Pinochet in response to a threat of invasion by the military government of Argentina that later turned its warlike energies in another direction. The section of southern Chile where the ocean penetrates the mountains and the coast becomes a maze of inlets and islands, begins just north of where the northern boundary of the Province of Chubut crosses Argentina.

The Pinochet highway runs from Chaiten (on the Pacific across the Andes from Esquel) to Coyaike some 400 kilometres farther south. There is a pass some 60 kilometres west of Esquel and another near Coyaike; we decided to make the round trip in 1986 with Moira who was coming to spend Christmas with us. By then all our daughters lived and worked in Buenos Aires.

She arrived on the 22nd of December and we set out in the pick up on the morning of the 23rd, lunched in the little town of Futuleufu, just across the border in Chile, and carried on westwards. Peaks broke through the temperate forest, hot springs rose among the coligüe, glaciers came to within an easy walk of the road and there were lakes and rivers of every colour, brilliant blue, dark green, turquoise, crystalline and chalky grey. We spent the night in a comfortable 'hosteria' in Chaiten with a view over the town and bay to a mountain that looked as if its top had been blown askew by the wind from the Pacific.

The next day, after a visit to hot baths in a cleft in a mountain just off the road, we drove back on our tracks to where the road that Pinochet had made in 1977, branched off to the south. It was sign posted 'camino de penetracón'. A man on the ferry that toiled across the neck of lake Yelcho −the engine was out of order- told us that he had a small farm in the area. Until the road was made he had to ride to Trevelin for provisions, a fifteen day trip there and back with pack horses.

As we turned into the southern branch at the fork a number of

168

wild looking figures leaped out from the side of the road signalling frantically.

"No, no, not four," said Charlie, braking. "Four is too many."

He stopped and got out of the pick up. A thin young man came up to the door on my side speaking unintelligible Spanish.

"Are you Australian?" asked Moira. He nodded.

"You cant refuse a lift to an Australian," she called across to her father; but he had already given way.

The hitch hikers were an a-typical Australian, a pale, dreamy youth who did not seem at all surprised to meet a fellow countryman in a part of the world where they are, in fact, rare. His rucksack with all he had in it had been stolen and he carried his belongings in two small, nylon carrier bags.. Then there was a Swiss; small, bouncey, efficient, a hitch hiker for the joy of it, he seemed to have more money than his companions. Finally there was an Israeli couple. Etty was small and dynamic; she had done her military service with the Israeli army as a paratrooper. Her husband, a big, strongly built young man, had a good tempered expression. As he spoke neither English nor Spanish all we could exchange with him were smiles.

Etty, who travelled in the cabin with us, told us in her incorrect, emphatic English that she and her husband had been waiting on that corner two days for a lift. They had been told that there was a bus service between Chaiten and Puerto Aisén but the bus, it seemed, only ran if there were enough passengers to justify the trip. They had got a lift on a truck going into Argentina and dropped off at the fork. After two days, she said gazing unbelievingly at the scenery moving past outside the windows, it felt as if you would never move again.

We lunched at three o'clock in the only village between the fork where we picked up the hitch hikers and Puyuguapi, where we intended to spend the night. We sat round a large table that only just fitted into a room behind a bar. All except Etty, who was vegetarian, ate indifferent meat and delicious tomatoes. Charlie addressed the hitch hikers by country, a form of address that had the advantage of attracting the subject's attention immediately. Even Israel, enveloped in a cloud of meaningless words, responded to his new name.

Charlie paid the bill, organised the party back into the pick up and drove on through the forest.

"Is your father a rich man?" asked Australia of Moira.

"No."

"He behaves like one."

That afternoon we lost time with ferries; it was half past six by the time we drove into Puyuguapi, a village of some six hundred people, scattered round the head of an inlet that wound in from the sea. We were almost among the houses before we made out where the long, narrow lake we had been following ended and the long, narrow inlet began.

In Chile the police are known as carabiñeros. At that time there was a police check point at which travellers must show their documents in every town and village. When ours had been approved we asked where we could spend the night and were directed to Doña Ursula. Her house stood in a garden full of trees and flowers sheltered from the inlet by a row of pines. It was a most attractive spot.

The house was being altered and Doña Ursula was in the nervous state that afflicts tidy minded women when their houses are full of workmen and wood shavings. When she asked how many we were and Moira, hoping for reduction in price, said seven her reaction was strongly negative. She could not possibly put up seven people with the state her house was in. After looking round Puyuguapi we went back and persuaded her to take the three of us. Her prices were too high for the hitch hikers anyhow.

Switzerland found himself a room with a shower and lent his tent to Australia who camped with the Israelis on a damp patch of grass at the head of the inlet. They looked very comfortable when we went to visit them in the late evening. Etty was writing up her diary, her hand moving from right to left across the page, while Israel with firm kindness kept a crowd of inquisitive children off the pile of rucksacks. We were warmly invited to join them in a cup of beef tea.

Earlier Moira and I had walked to the store to buy a bottle of whiskey. Imported whiskey was much cheaper in Chile than in Argentina at that time. The store was a big building made, as are most buildings in that part of Chile, banks and churches as well as private homes, of wood. To one side was the jetty at which the coastal steamers that served Pujuguapi and other towns along the coast, tied up, on the other a carpet factory where the girls were just getting up from their looms. We climbed the steps to the entrance of the store and found ourselves in a big room with a counter across the width. Our side was crowded with people, among them Australia. Moira offered to interpret but he had already contacted an English speaker, one of the owners, with whom he was slowly and softly debating the price of a bottle of wine.

It was eleven o'clock and we were very hungry before Doña Ursula let us know that dinner was ready. It was easily the best meal we had in Chile. Hard boiled eggs in a sauce, set on lettuce leaves and sprinkled with chives, were followed by smoked fish with a salad of potatoes, onions and pickles dressed with mayonnaise. To accompany the food we had a bottle of white wine. Only the apricots that ended the meal were out of a tin. The inlet provided the fish and Doña Ursula smoked it.

The hitch hikers were waiting for us beside the pick up next morning. After wishing each other a Merry Christmas we set off, quite forgetting a folder with the car papers, our entry permits into Chile and other essential documents that remained lying on a shelf on one of the many pieces of furniture in our bedroom. It was a lovely morning and we drove slowly along a narrow road that wound along the shore of the inlet, stopping to watch dolphins leaping and diving close by. As the scenery unfolded Etty chatted about life as a paratrooper and the smell of death in Beirut; about how she missed her mother and father and about their party the night before.

A family from one of the houses near their tents had invited them to join their Christmas Eve celebrations. Moira and I questioned her eagerly but Etty's English was more suited to conveying facts than local colour, and her background knowledge of South America was limited. Her worst moment had been the arrival of a large cake that was probably flavoured with some sort of liqueur. 'It was not a nice cake'. But those kindly people of Puyuguapi for whom, no doubt, a cake was an unusual treat, made sure their guests had liberal helpings. Switzerland was a favourite with the girls and danced all night. As it was apparently country dancing, 'they danced as if they were on horse back', he must have been a quick learner. Australia kept hurrying to the door and playing a torch over the tents to make sure that no one was making off with heir belongings.

The road turned away from the inlet into a valley. The forest became even thicker, the road narrower, peaks closed in ahead. When it could go no farther the road began to climb the side of the valley, up and up in close curves until we were almost level with the snowfield opposite. Where we stopped to look at the view the tree trunks were splashed with red where a tiny creeper produced patches of minute, elongated flowers. The undergrowth had thinned and the forest was full of humming birds. Over the top we came on a glacier, a layer of blueish ice that capped a wall of rock. From between the ice and the rock a column of water poured into invisible depths. Lower down we stopped to admire the beautiful river Cisnes flowing between rocks worn smooth by water.

About here Charlie discovered the loss of the folder of papers which would give endless trouble to replace in Argentina, even if we were allowed out of Chile without them. At the next town, the first that morning, we looked eagerly for the police stop. For the first time since entering Chile we found it unmanned and remembered that it was Christmas Day. We were directed to the police station where we were attended by a young man, smart and well shaven as were the carabiñeros everywhere, but with a Christmassy gleam in his eye. He promised to speak to the carabiñeros in Puyuguapi by radio that afternoon and have our papers sent on to Coyaike, where we intended to spend the night, by the first available transport. As we had met only two cars all morning and the bus was not running regularly we did not feel hopeful of being in Esquel next day as we had planned.

It was after three o'clock when we reached Puerto Aisén; no longer a port since the earthquake of 1960 raised that stretch of coast. At the service station, where we were given a Christmas parcel −a calendar, some toys and sweets- we asked for a good restaurant. We were directed to a nice looking place in a different category from the one where we had lunched the previous day. When we got out of the car the hitch hikers announced that the meal was on them. My heart bled for them as it was obvious that the price was going to be in a different category too.

There were still a number of diners in the pleasant low ceilinged room where we had our Christmas lunch. We sat at a well laid table with a white clothe and napkins, some of us a bit scruffy but all very much at home. After a good deal of thought and consultation of the price column on the menu the hovering waitresses were able to note down our various choices. Nothing much of anything was left by the end of the meal.

After lunch we parted; they to go their various ways about the tip of South America while we headed inland to Coyaike. We found our papers in a sealed envelope at the police station next morning. We were not allowed to pay for the trouble we had caused. I hope Doña Ursula received my letter of apology and thanks.

Glossary

Aguada: watering place.

Araucano: race indigenous to South America.

Araucano: language spoken by Araucanos.

Araucaria: (araucaria araucano) Monkey puzzle tree.

Asador: iron stake on which meat is threaded before being stuck in the ground and leaned over a fire to cook.

Bastos: the base for a recado.

Bolas perdidas: variety of boleadora made with one stone only.

Boleadoras: rounded stones, usually three, joined by rawhide thongs; thrown when hunting in such a way as to wrap themselves around the legs of the quarry.

Cabecillo: head of ritual in a camaruco.

Camaruco: ceremonial gathering of indigenous people.

Carabiñeros: Chilean police.

Charqui: meat that has been salted and dried.

Chicha: alcoholic drink made by fermenting apples.

Ciprés: (austrocedrus chilensis) conifer native to the Andes.

Coihue: (nothrofagus dombeyi) magnificent evergreen tree native to the Andes in the provinces of Neuquen, Rio Negro and Chubut and corresponding areas in Chile.

Coligüe: cane that grows in the central ranges of the Andes.

Cuis: small mammal similar to a guinea pig.

Fiestas: the Christmas/New Year party season.

Fortín: defensive post made to keep the Indians out of the settled areas.

Maiten: (maitenus boaria) stately evergreen tree native to the Andes in the provinces of Neuquen, Rio Negro and Chubut and corresponding areas in Chile.

Malacara: horse with a broad white blaze down its face.

Maneas: rawhide strap for hobbling horses.

Manzaneros: people from Las Manzanas.

Mapuches: a group within the Araucano people.

Modai: a drink made from fermented wheat.

Neneo: round prickly bush that grows in the pre-Cordillera.

Pehuenches: central figures in the ritual of the camaruco.

Pifilca: whistle made from a section of the stem of a dry hemlock or from a guanaco bone.

Piñones: fruit of the araucaria.

Tehuelches: race indigenous to Patagonia.

Tejuela: wooden tile for roofing.

Toldería: tent village; a collection of tents.

Torta frita: a sort of damper.

Travesía: desert crossing.

Trutruca: primitive musical instrument made with coligüe canes and a horn.